KEEPING SCORE

Keeping Score: Strategies and Tactics for Winning the Quality War

Perry L. Johnson

1817

Harper & Row, Publishers, New York
BALLINGER DIVISION

*Grand Rapids, Philadelphia, St. Louis, San Francisco
London, Singapore, Sydney, Tokyo, Toronto*

International Standard Book Number: 0–88730–385–4

Library of Congress Catalog Card Number:

Printed in the United States of America

Library of Congress Cataloging-in-Publication Data

Johnson, Perry L. (Perry Lawrence), 1948-
    Keeping score : strategies and tactics for winning the quality war / Perry L. Johnson
      p. cm.
    ISBN 0–88730–385–4
    1. Quality control. 2. Quality assurance. I. Title.
TS156.J655 1989   89-37892
   658.5'62-dc20   CIP

89 90 91 92 HD 9 8 7 6 5 4 3 2 1

Contents

Introduction

A mountain of spark plugs!

That's how the TV ad opened.

I stared in disbelief as the camera panned across those huge piles of plugs . . . spread out as far as the eye could see.

The ad was from one of the world's leading industrial firms. And these, the ad said, were defective plugs: rejects, hundreds of thousands of them.

These bad plugs had been caught by the plug maker's rigid inspection procedures and safely discarded to make sure we customers got only good plugs.

Quality is a tough business, the ad said. But, it added proudly, we're committed to it. No effort is too great; no expense is too staggering.

As a portrayal of "quality in the eighties," this ad was fascinating not so much for what it said as for what it didn't say.

The ad didn't mention the defective plugs that must have eluded the plug maker's inspection process. No such process is perfect. Even when you inspect everything two or three different times, defects still slip through. Those would end up in someone's car—maybe mine.

The ad didn't mention the fact that an inspection process tends to overlook products of marginal quality, plugs that "seem okay" at inspection but perform poorly later. Those,too,would end up in someone's car—maybe mine, maybe even yours.

The ad didn't mention how expensive the inspection procedures are. Manufacturers spend millions of dollars for inspectors and equipment whose mission in life is to tell them how bad they're doing. Who pays for that? You and I do.

The ad didn't mention the cost of the discarded, "defective" plugs. Who covers that cost? You know who.

Then there's the expense of the ad itself. The creative, production and media costs had to amount to a small fortune— all for a firm to brag not about its quality, but about its utter *lack* of quality: "Look at all the bad plugs we make!"

But the plug maker wasn't unique in its ignorance of what quality is or how to deliver it. That same ignorance led American business down from the peak of world economic leadership to the dark days of 1979–1981, a time when it seemed that American manufacturing was finished.

Steel companies closed plants and diversified frantically to stay alive. Hearths in Youngstown, Bethlehem, and elsewhere went cold for the first time in 70 years.

Chrysler Corporation, facing extinction, prepared to beg for federal loan guarantees. The move was unprecedented, controversial, and humiliating.

Ford Motor Company had taken a record $5.5 billion in losses over three years. The gush of red ink flowed freely. Ford's lines of credit began to run dry. Under the relentless pressure of foreign competitors, its back was to the wall.

The United States seemed poised to lose its position as the world's leading industrial and economic power. Stagnation and malaise were the order of the day—a sorry sight, especially when you consider the unquestioned leadership American business enjoyed in an earlier era.

I call that era, which ended about 1950, the Invention Age. It was an exciting era, one that was almost uniquely American; for when you name an invention from the period 1850 to 1950, its creator was usually American: Samuel Morse's telegraph, Charles Pillsbury's white flour, the Wright Brothers' airplane, Elias Howe's sewing machine, Elisha Otis's elevator, Cyrus McCormick's cultivator, Richard Gatling's machine gun, Henry Ford's engine and automotive assembly line, Thomas Edison's light bulb and just-about-everything-else.

People like these, along with Carnegie, Rockefeller, Armour, and many others, came from diverse backgrounds and pursued different dreams. Yet they had several key things in common. They were American: intensely creative, fiercely ambitious, courageous. Their intuition enabled them to discern people's needs, and their creativity enabled them to satisfy those needs.

These inventors and innovators, along with many others, bequeathed America a century of world economic dominance. During the Invention Age, "Made in America" was the most powerful endorsement going. American business could do little wrong; it created vast wealth for a few and an unheard-of standard of living for many.

Success in those days depended on *invention,* rather than *refinement;* uniqueness made up for many shortcomings. People bought Model T Fords in 1909 because they were uniquely economical and durable. This made up for an inexplicable shifting mechanism, the difficulty (and very real danger) of crank starting, the limitations on muddy and icy roads, and the somewhat restricted color selection. It was enough merely to have a car.

People bought Dumont television sets in 1948 because they were unique. This made up for the tiny screen; the atrocious sound; the snowy, blurred picture; and the limited programming. It was enough merely to have a TV.

Model Ts and Dumonts are, of course, long gone. Refinement—a never-ending game of "Can you top this?"— has pushed them into museums. It's no longer a thrill merely to have a car or a TV.

Cars and TVs are no longer made by small firms driven by eccentric geniuses like "Crazy Henry" Ford. They're made by conglomerates—dozens, even hundreds, worldwide.

That same scenario, played out with virtually every other consumer product and service, signaled the end of the Invention Age and the dawn of a new one that I call the Quality Age. And the Quality Age brought with it three new realities.

Reality One: Reduced Pace and Impact of Invention

Compare the advances of the Invention Age with the list of inventions introduced since then. The electronics industry has given us the computer, the videocassette recorder, video games, compact discs, electronic pagers, and smoke detectors. The space program has blessed us with Teflon and Velcro. Other inventions include disposable diapers and hand-held calculators.

Arguably, many of these are innovations, not inventions. They're all worthwhile, but can we realistically say that they've had as fundamental an impact on average American consumers as did the pre–1950 inventions? Look at it this way. Given a choice, would you give up light bulbs and automobiles or VCRs and Velcro? There's no contest.

The Quality Age is, indeed, an age of innovation, not invention. By that I mean no disrespect to the achievements of today's innovators. Daily, they introduce enhancements of products and services that make our lives just a little bit better.

My point is that, in this Quality Age, we cannot invent our way to health and success. Health and success depend on our ability to make existing products and services better. Stagnant firms haven't grasped that reality yet.

Reality Two: Me-Toomanship

During the Invention Age, there was virtually no such thing as a world market. That is a function of the Quality Age. Where there once were two, four, or half a dozen competitors for a given product or service, there can now be dozens or hundreds, thanks to our shrunken world.

In this crowded marketplace, no innovation is exclusive for long. This is the "me-too" era. Competitors watch each other like hawks, matching refinements feature for feature in a never-ending and confusing game of one-upmanship. If your competitor adds a bell, you add a whistle. If his lights are green, you make yours amber. If she says hers tastes good, you say yours tastes great. If all else fails, call your product "new and improved."

And on the rare occasion when a firm offers a product or service that really is unique, there are always potential competitors poised to lunge out of the woodwork with a cheaper, and sometimes even better, version. The perpetrator calls this an "enhancement." The victim calls it a "knockoff."

Some companies make a living at this type of activity. They allow the innovator to make the expensive mistakes, to create the market and sometimes even the need, before bringing out their competitive version. Japanese companies are particularly adept at this tactic—patiently refining their version of an existing product, then coming out and killing you with it. Even IBM employed this strategy in 1980 with the introduction of its PC.

Competition in product/service features is exacerbated by competition in distribution and marketing methods. In this Quality Age, thanks to private labeling, product licensing, the multiplicity of media, and the science of demographics, a virtually identical product can be sold under myriad disguises by many flavors of marketers.

As a result of all this, the Quality Age marketplace is a vast arena of products and services competing on a virtual parity basis. Ecclesiastes' ancient dictum "There is nothing new under the sun" was never truer.

This has created the most significant reality of the Quality Age.

Reality Three: A Wary, Jaded Consumer

Today's consumers are overwhelmed with choices. They're aware of the virtual parities in pricing and features of most products and services. And they've developed a healthy skepticism of benefit claims. They know of only one attribute that can vary tremendously, and they make their choices based on their assessment of that attribute: quality.

Uniqueness and novelty are virtually gone. *Quality* has become the yardstick, the great differentiator, the chief basis upon which today's consumers judge competing products.

Where at one time merely "having" something—like a car— was sufficient, it is no longer.

Consumers no longer go to "the" grocery. Confronted with choices, they select a grocery that, by comparison, is cleaner, better lighted; one that offers convenient hours and a wide selection; one that will cash checks without Justice Department clearance; one that employs courteous, helpful people.

Consumers have become aware of their power. If visits to "the" doctor are marked by long waits, inattentiveness, sloppy billing, missed or broken appointments, and discourteous, unhelpful treatment, they try someone else.

Consumers may not expect haute cuisine at a fast-burger outlet. Still, when they are made to wait interminably, are served cold food, or get surly treatment, they can always try the outlet on the next block—and usually do.

Today's consumers base quality judgments on personal experience and word-of-mouth, and they do so almost reflexively. No customers, whether they've bought from you once or a hundred times, can be taken for granted. You're fighting a host of others for the consumer's dollar with every move you make. The consumer's stance toward you is "What have you done for me lately?" You're only as good as your last transaction. If you don't make the cut, you're out. Period.

You may have the "best price." You may be "number one" in your market. Your company may have "been around forever." Big deal. What you think doesn't matter. What matters is that your customers know your product or service is not unique. There's no law requiring anyone to buy from you.

What makes people buy from you? Your ability to meet or exceed their expectations. And that takes more than putting up a few signs.

- It requires the conscious and continuing will to do so.
- It requires the consistent gathering and evaluation of feedback from the entire universe of customers, competitors, and suppliers.
- It requires constant improvement and refinement of all aspects of the operation.

What we're talking about is a living, breathing, dynamic system—a Quality Age system.

Quality Age Firms

In America today, there are many Quality Age firms. Many of these bear household names. And, as I see it, they fall into two categories.

The first I call *sustainers*. While virtually every firm is at least *born* with energy and dynamism, sustainers have somehow managed to renew those qualities constantly as time goes on.

One example of a sustainer is the International Business Machines Corporation. In its over 60-year history, IBM has dominated virtually every field it has entered, from office typewriters to midrange computers and word processors. In a history notable for its lack of major missteps, Big Blue has become a global giant.

One example IBM's ability to improve and refine goes back to the days before the dawn of the Quality Age. In the early 1930s, IBM introduced an electric typewriter to be used as a billing machine in accounting departments. This was hardly unique. Electric typewriters themselves had been sold since before the turn of the century, and IBM was by this time only one of a host of electric typewriter makers.

Given all that, sales of IBM's billing machine were surprisingly strong. In an effort to find out why the machine was selling so well, IBM representatives talked to their customers and were shocked to learn that the typewriter wasn't being used as a billing machine at all! Instead it was being used as a general office typewriter for letters, reports, and other materials because customers found it was easy to operate, reliable, and able to produce excellent print quality. In these respects, it was far superior to competing general office typewriters.

IBM heard only one complaint: because the typewriter was intended for use as a billing machine, it only typed in upper case. IBM lost no time modifying the typewriter to produce both upper and lower case—and took the typewriter market by storm.

A more recent example of IBM's ability to improve, refine, and meet customer expectations occurred in 1980, when it introduced its first personal computer. This was, like the typewriter, not an invention. Commodore and others had been marketing PCs for several years. So IBM faced competition going in.

There were other problems too. The personal computer in general was regarded as a novelty, a plaything, a "solution looking for a problem." Plus, the personal computer market was thought to be well off IBM's turf. Experts noted these problems and speculated that Big Blue had, at last, tripped on its own feet.

In retrospect, their move was obviously brilliant. IBM let others bear the expense of creating the market and the expense of the product development mistakes. Then IBM communicated its image for quality and its image as a computer maker (interestingly, many people thought IBM was in the PC business several years before it actually entered it) to markets it had never entered before. In the process, IBM's PC became not just a best-seller but also the industry standard: the epitome of competitive performance.

Certainly, no firm is perfect. But, as a classic sustainer, IBM learned from its blunders and was clearly a Quality Age firm before it had to be. It refines, it improves, it sustains.

The other form of Quality Age company is the *rebounder*, a firm that has come back from the brink of extinction to survive and excel. The best example of a rebounder is the Ford Motor Company. In 1980, as I mentioned, its condition was nightmarish. Yet, in 1986 alone, it earned a record 3.28 billion dollars. Even more remarkable, in that year Ford out-earned its gigantic arch-rival General Motors for the first time since 1924.

Clearly, this was no fluke. Ford beat its own profit record in 1987 and was on track to beat it yet again in 1988. It had gone from death-rattle to dominance in less than a decade. Talk about rebound!

Like the other automakers, Ford cut its payroll. But, unlike General Motors, Ford made little investment in robotics or other Star Wars technologies. Unlike Chrysler, Ford made no major divestitures. Instead, Ford reinvented itself with energy, dynamism, and a never-ending effort to meet its customers' expectations. This is the trademark of the Quality Age firm.

Then there are all the others: firms in stasis or decline. They work hard but don't get anywhere; they feel competitive breath on their necks but reassure themselves with slogans like "stay the course" and "if it ain't broke, don't fix it."

Their prospects for the future are not bright. The scenario looks like this: of the 1975 Fortune 500, two-fifths are booming, two-fifths are gone, and one-fifth hangs in the balance. I expect that cycle to repeat itself before the 1990s are out.

Perhaps you think that your firm belongs to that middle group—the one that may not be around in 10 years. Maybe you're afraid that the situation is hopeless. Maybe you've given up any idea of rebounding. All I can say is, *the situation is never hopeless. It's never too late to rebound.*

Look, for example, at Chrysler Motors. In 1980 the firm was in even more dire trouble than Ford. Everyone said Chrysler was doomed; no one thought it would pull out. But pull out it did—and *not*, despite the popular myth, due to a "government bailout." Not only did the government not bail Chrysler out, the government actually made a windfall profit on its loan guarantees!

Chrysler survived and entered its era of excellence by getting back to the basics. Many other firms—some in dire trouble, some merely stagnant, even many doing well—are trying to do the same by improving quality and productivity, involving workers, getting closer to the customer.

This movement has an explosive growth in the quality field: books on quality, courses on quality, and theory upon theory upon theory.

Back when I was a Fortune 100 executive, our president tried to improve quality by issuing a letter to all employees. In it, he stated that the firm's problems had become intolerable. He was, therefore, enacting a new policy: "zero defects." By following this policy and committing no defects, we would have quality from now on. End of letter. End of policy.

This edict did not meet with wholehearted acceptance by the workforce. "Zero defects?" they grumbled. "How does he expect us to do that? Does he think we make defects on purpose?"

The zero defects approach belongs to what I call the *motivational family* of quality improvement strategies. This family of methods is characterized by slogans, pep rallies, banners, pens, cups, and other trinkets. The idea is that if everyone is motivated to think quality, then quality will happen.

I'll be the first to insist that motivation is a key ingredient of improvement, but motivation alone does not work. Such programs are like Halley's Comet: They're all sound and fury for a few days, and then things go back to the way they were for 76 more years.

J. M. Juran, a leading quality/productivity expert for over a half century, describes "zero defects" as a "banner to fly during a company drive to improve quality. . . . If the drive is ill-conceived (e.g., an attempt to solve the company's quality problems by exhorting the workforce), then it will fail no matter how clever the slogan."[1]

Rivaling the motivational family of improvement plans is the *scientific approach*. This consists of an entire array of statistical and mathematical formulas, usually devised by professors for professors, taught to the unwary in lengthy classroom sessions. The idea is that if everyone applies these formulas on the job, then quality will happen.

I'm a statistician myself, and I firmly believe that statistical methods are a key to improvement. But they can't do the job alone. Such programs are like a root canal: dreaded, endured, and forgotten as quickly as possible.

Firms try these techniques in good faith. Their hearts are in the right place. They want to improve; they want desperately to improve. The problem is that they lack the necessary tools.

In my consulting practice, I've seen firms of all types— manufacturing, service, government—apply both types of improvement methods. I've observed that most popular "quality/productivity improvement" plans attack only the symptoms, rather than the cause: stagnation and malaise.

I've found that the most effective approach—the one used by today's Quality Age firms—relies not on motivation or science, but *combines* them.

The approach, which I call Integrated Quality Management, (IQM), uses motivation and science—a specific set of proven tools—to bring a whole new attitude to the organization, an attitude of never-ending improvement.

How does IQM do this?

IQM Puts Quality into Practical Perspective

With IQM, we define quality, generally, as giving customers what they want. That sounds simple, but it's much more than a slogan. "What customers want" can be maddeningly vague, often contradictory, and it constantly changes; moreover, learning what they want is one thing, reacting to it effectively is quite another.

IQM also puts major emphasis on the *perception* of quality. To stagnant firms, "perception" and "image" are advertising terms. To Quality Age firms, the *perception* of quality is as important as intrinsic quality, and the *image* of quality is a priceless asset. Quality Age firms know that a poor quality image costs dearly, while a good quality image is the best advertising of all.

How do we learn what customers want? How do we take that message into our system and respond effectively? How do we maintain and build our quality image. This book shows you how Quality Age firms do it.

IQM Replaces Stagnation with Energy and Dynamism

Business organizations are composed of people. People instinctively fear change, and therefore, so do businesses. The fear of change and the refusal to face or deal with change cause stagnation. Inertia, another common human trait, perpetuates it.

How do we break the inertia? How do we create a system within our firms that expects change, responds to it, even *forces* it? This books shows you how Quality Age firms do it.

IQM Puts Simple, Scientific Scorekeeping Techniques in Place

Our businesses have science in their labs and scorekeeping in their financials. But they quite often have neither anyplace else. Yet scorekeeping is not the antithesis of motivation; it is what makes motivation effective. Scorekeeping unites the organization by showing us where we've been, how we're doing, and where we're going. Effective scorekeeping involves the work force of all types and at all levels in ways that nothing else can.

Effective scorekeeping teaches quality as nothing else can; effective scorekeeping attacks stagnation as nothing else can. Effective scorekeeping is at the heart of every Quality Age firm. And keeping score is ultimately what this book is all about.

Integrated Quality Management is more than a slogan or a formula; it's a complete quality/productivity improvement plan that works. It's built around seven solid, proven principles, which are being followed by Ford, Amoco, Johnson Wax, and other Quality Age firms. IQM will work for you, too; today, into the nineties, and beyond.

To the pioneers in excellence:
yesterday, today, and tomorrow

KEEPING SCORE

PART I

THE ROLES OF QUALITY

Aside from competitive strength, what are the differences between today's stagnant firms and today's thriving Quality Age firms? I'll be pointing out these differences throughout this book. But for now, let's sum them up with a comment from Dr. W. Edwards Deming, a quality/productivity expert whose guidance played a major role in Japan's postwar recovery:

> It is no longer sufficient to have the customer not complain. It is necessary, for good business, to have customers that boast about your product or service, stay with you, and bring in a friend for new business.[2]

Quality Age firms strive for customers who boast. Stagnant firms settle for minimizing customer complaints. And most stagnant firms don't even do that very well.

A good example is the spark plug maker I mentioned in the introduction. This company's aim was to minimize customer complaints; its strategy was to *inspect defects out*. The aim of a Quality Age spark plug maker would be to make its customers boast; its strategy would be to *build quality in*.

There's quite a difference between the two approaches and quite a challenge as well.

"Building quality in" reminds me of the analogy a NASA scientist used to describe the precision needed to get a spaceship to the moon. He said it was like trying to throw a softball into a mailbox while riding a bicycle at full speed. That's due to the awesome forces of change constantly at work. The earth revolves both on its axis and around the sun; at the same time, the moon revolves around the earth.

Similar awesome forces of change are at work in and around our firms. Customers change; processes change; supplied products and services change. There are political forces, competitive forces, cultural forces, natural forces.

These forces of change affect stagnant and Quality Age firms alike. The difference lies in the way the firms deal with those forces.

Stagnant firms dread change. They hope that if they ignore it, it will go away. With such an attitude, the best they can ever do is try to inspect defects out—a hopeless cause. Quality Age firms not only accept change, they are also on the constant lookout for it. They're not only prepared to deal with it, they exploit it, sometimes even *force* it themselves when it's to their advantage.

That sort of dynamism allows Quality Age firms to go far beyond inspecting defects out. They're able to build quality in and create customers who boast.

They're able to "build quality in" because they know what quality really is in our dynamic, ever-changing world. They view it not as an end-of-the-line concept, but as a reality that plays major roles in every component of their business: their customers, their process, and their suppliers.

1

Quality:
Myths and Realities

The terms *quality* and *beauty* have one thing in common: There are as many definitions of them as there are definers.

The dictionary defines *beauty* as "that which gives pleasure to the senses or pleasurably exalts the mind or spirit." That's fine—but it does not explain how the term beauty can be seriously ascribed to things as disparate as Elvis and Brahms, Bauhaus and Mesopotamian architecture, attitude art and art deco, the smell of a rose and the smell of napalm, the Bugatti Royale and the VW Bug.

Defining *quality* is just as slippery. The dictionary defines it as "excellence; superiority." Corporate accountants, looking at the cost of rectifying customer dissatisfaction as well as the costs of motivational and training programs, define quality as "expensive." Others insist that quality is free.[3]

Some say that quality is meeting customer requirements. Others maintain that quality is giving customers what they want. Still others have narrowed it further by defining quality as "functionality and durability at a fair price," and it's even been said that the inverse of quality is the "loss imparted to society."[4]

In these quality-conscious 1980s, it seems that everyone has taken a shot at defining quality, but no definition has been adopted by acclamation. This maddening, nebulous seven-letter word has become, for many, just another buzz term of the 1980s.

Stagnant firms remain bound up by a network of myths about quality, which they accept as gospel. Quality Age firms look at quality a different way. To them, it's not a buzz term; it's the *imperative* of the 1990s. It's not just a slogan or a toy for wordsmiths, but a living, breathing, dynamic way of life.

What are the quality myths? What are the realities?

Myth 1: Quality Is a Technically Perfect Product or Service

Same Product, Different Suppliers

A certain fastener maker started having quality problems a while back. These problems grew till a major client, one of the Big Three automakers, quit doing business with the fastener firm altogether.

This forced the fastener maker's top managers to confront their quality problems. They implemented a quality improvement program, and their efforts paid off. The quality of their product improved so dramatically that they approached their former customer about resuming their business relationship.

"Nothing doing," the automaker said. "We don't like your quality."

The fastener maker did not give up. Its representative submitted samples of its product to the automaker. "Check our quality now," they said. "See for yourself."

"Sorry, but no sale," was the automaker's response.

This was frustrating beyond belief. The fastener maker had, through a great deal of effort, made a genuine turnaround. Its managers now felt that its quality was unsurpassed in the industry. Yet the automaker was like a stone wall.

They cast about for a solution and finally found one. The fastener firm was on amicable terms with a distributor that regularly did business with the Big Three, including the firm that had been the fastener maker's former customer. A deal was cut. "Here's our product," the fastener maker said to the distributor. "You go sell it to the car company."

The distributor offered the fasteners to the automaker, submitted samples for evaluation, and got the business.

Same fasteners, different supplier.

You'd think that the fastener company would have succeeded in resuming its relationship with the automaker once it had improved the intrinsic quality of its product. But that would be true only if we lived in a world of robots who lack feelings and perceptions, in a world where intrinsic quality was all there is to quality.

But we live in a world of people with thoughts, feelings, and perceptions. And intrinsic quality is not all there is to quality. The *perception of quality* is a vital element too. It's as important—maybe even more so—than intrinsic quality.

When the automaker determined that the fasteners were of poor quality, something else happened. The automaker developed a *perception* that the fastener maker's quality was poor. This perception withstood the fastener maker's most earnest efforts to demonstrate its improved quality.

Finally, the automaker accepted the very same fasteners through a third party. Nothing had changed but the supplier. The automaker took the fasteners because its *perception* of the third party's quality was good. Same product, different perceptions.

Same Company, Different Cars

Let's look at the same issue on a broader scale by comparing the Ford Edsel of the late 1950s with the Ford Taurus/ Mercury Sable of the early 1980s. The parallels are striking. So are the contrasts.

Both projects were major capital undertakings for Ford. Both came along during troubled times for the auto industry. Both were brand-new designs from platform to greenhouse. Both possessed significant technological innovations; both possessed looks that insiders felt were risky and daring, to say the least. Both cars were introduced with all the fanfare Ford could muster. Both shipped well at first. Both were plagued with various sorts of defects during the introduction year, problems that Ford fixed by the second model year.

And the contrasts? The first is obvious. The Taurus and Sable have been sales blockbusters. On the list of factors that helped Ford rebound, these cars are at or near the top. Yet the Edsel not only died an ignominious death, the name has become to "failure" what Kleenex is to "tissues."

There's one other contrast between these two cars that is seldom, if ever, noted. The Taurus and Sable were introduced several years after Ford began pounding its "Quality is Job 1" advertising theme into the consciousnesses of American car buyers. The Edsel did not have the benefit of such a campaign.

Does this contrast help explain the outcome of the two product launches? I think so. We're talking about *perception* once again.

For all Ford's talk about quality, the Taurus and Sable experienced quality problems typical of many new model launches. But the public, it seems, was willing to overlook or forgive those problems because it perceived Ford as a quality company. Such forgiveness was obviously not forthcoming for the Edsel. But then, Ford was not at that time perceived as a quality company.

What if the public *had* perceived Ford as a quality firm in 1957? What would have happened to the Edsel, had Ford's quality image been as good then as it had become by 1983? This is only conjecture, but it's conceivable that, if Ford's quality image had been better, the Edsel's "horse-collar" grille and horizontal fins might have been perceived as stylistic breakthroughs. The look might have become trendy.

Instead, the Edsel was perceived as ugly and earned various derisive nicknames, of which "Ethel" was the kindest. Perception versus fact. Illusion versus reality.

"What It Is" Is What You Think It Is

The power of perception is visible in many areas of our lives. Consumer researchers have long noticed that rankings or opinions of products can vary dramatically depending on what the subjects are told. Take "taste tests," for example. Subjects taste a selection of competing products without being told who made them; they rank the products according to taste. Then the same subjects taste the same selection of competing products—only now they're told who made them. The subjects rank the products differently! The difference between the two tests is simply a matter of perception.

This occurs in medical testing, too. Subjects who share an ailment are given a medication. That is, two-thirds of the subjects get medication; the other third unknowingly gets a placebo. Invariably, many of the placebo subjects report an improvement in their symptoms. They believe they'll get better, so they do. It's the power of perception.

Remember when "made in Japan" was a slur? For years, it seemed, all Japanese products were tarred with same brush. Surely not everything made in Japan was junk, but people certainly assumed it was. "Made in Japan" was all they needed to know.

All that has certainly changed, and not just because the Japanese have dramatically improved their intrinsic quality. They've also placed continuing emphasis on improving the *perception* their customers have of their quality. One example of this is the phenomenon called *fit and finish*, a term unknown in the American auto lexicon till Japanese imports began to arrive. Suddenly Japanese fit and finish was all the rage. The paint looked good, the panels fit tight, the trim was even and uniform.

While good fit and finish has some bearing on intrinsic quality, it has more to do with the perception of quality; customers assumed that the external quality they could see was evidence of internal quality they couldn't see. And the Japanese began taking a serious market share from U.S. automakers such as Ford.

Ford's market share was ripe for the taking in the late 1970s. It had horrendous problems with intrinsic quality, including constant recalls, outer body rust-through, exploding Pintos. The people at Ford knew that. And like concerned managers in many other firms, they began a program to correct them. But unlike the well-meaning reformers in many other firms, whose quality consciousness begins and ends with intrinsic quality, the Ford team knew that improving intrinsic quality was not enough. They also had to improve the public's *perception* of quality—Ford's quality image.

So, in 1981, Ford began its "Quality is Job 1" campaign. Keep in mind that this was before any of its intrinsic quality initiatives had got off the ground. At the time Ford began the campaign, quality was only a promise, not a reality.

But Ford pressed on, driving the message home on TV and in print. Gradually, the public began to perceive Ford as a company committed to quality. At the same time, as Ford's quality improvement programs began to work, Ford gathered improved customer ratings and began to trumpet that information in its "Quality is Job 1" messages as well.

Ford's turnaround is due as much to improved quality image as it is to improvement in intrinsic product quality. So too are the rising fortunes of Chrysler, where Lee Iacocca has made a very personal, public, and effective issue of his firm's quality image. These and other firms prove that providing a technically perfect product or service isn't all there is to quality. What's just as important—if not more so—is the quality image.

Just an Illusion?

To many, the word "image" means the same thing as "illusion." But a good quality image is not an illusion. It does not come by magic. It is a hard, cold reality, a product of intense and continuous work that rewards its possessor with substantial benefits.

A good quality image *causes the occasional "sin" to be forgiven.* Strive though we might for perfection, we are, in fact, human. We can't help but make the occasional mistake. Every now and then we'll fail to deliver the pizza within the promised 30 minutes. We'll transpose two digits of an account number. We'll ship a size seven instead of a size nine. We'll lose a reservation. Zero defects, in a world populated by human beings, is an empty ideal.

A good quality image compensates for those occasional errors. When your customers *perceive* your quality as good, they will tend to dismiss your errors as flukes. They will tend not to be on the lookout for problems and will shrug off the problems that do occur: "These things happen."

A bad quality image, on the other hand, creates a whole set of unnecessary problems. Your customers and prospects will be suspicious and wary. They'll watch you closely, looking for problems, expecting the worst. They'll react to problems with an attitude of self-justification: "See? I knew it all along!" This attitude generates a vicious cycle that, if left unchecked, can destroy your business.

A good quality image *helps create repeat business*. It's what Deming is talking about when he challenges us to strive for customers who boast. A bad quality image is what causes customers to complain not just to us, but to their friends.

A good quality image *helps generate referral business*. Those boasting customers will, as Deming says, "bring in a friend for new business." Those aware of our bad quality image will, in fact, warn others away from us.

A good quality image *makes our advertising more efficient*. It is, in fact, a form of advertising itself, powerful beyond comprehension and absolutely free. A bad quality image works at cross-purposes to our advertising. It forces us to increase advertising spending to maintain volume and generate growth.

A good quality image is not just a nice thing to have, not when you consider the realities of the Quality Age that we talked about before. Given today's heavy competition among parity products and services; given today's instantaneous communication; given a population that is getting older, wiser, and better educated, a good quality image is essential.

Quality Age firms recognize all these facts. They prize their good quality image and consider it as important an asset as any other on their balance sheets: plant and equipment, inventory, accounts receivable, and all the rest.

Unfortunately, stagnant firms don't see it that way. To them, quality is a technically perfect product or service. Therefore, they aim all improvement efforts at the elimination of defects. Image, to them, is not a quality issue, but an advertising issue. But a good advertising alone cannot create a good quality image. Neither can a technically perfect product or service. There's much more to it than that.

The Flukes

One day a few years ago I was touring a plant that made wiring harness for aircraft engines. I worked the line from front to back, making notes. At the end were the inspectors, and I stopped to watch them.

One particular harness had a sealed connection that had to be strong enough to withstand 30 foot pounds of stress without breaking. To make sure that the connections were being made strong enough, an inspector was assigned to perform tests. Since the only way to test a connection was to break it, all the harnesses could not be tested. Instead, the inspector would pull five sample harnesses each hour, test these with a tensile strength tester, and then record the results.

I watched the inspector as she picked her five samples and took them to the tensile strength tester. She put the first harness on the tester and began to apply force. The harness stretched, strained, and finally snapped at the connection. The inspector read the dial—31 foot pounds—and wrote it down in her log. So far, so good.

The second sample took 34 foot pounds. Fine. The third sample broke at 27 foot pounds. Oddly, she did not write that reading down. She tossed the broken harness aside and went on to the next sample.

The fourth sample broke at 32. She wrote that down. The fifth took only 18 to break. She did not write that reading down; she put the harness aside.

Now she was out of samples. No problem; she went back to the line and pulled some more.

The sixth harness tested out at 36. She wrote that down. The seventh harness tested at 15. She put it aside. The next took 40; she wrote it down. The ninth sample broke at 26, and she discarded it without recording the reading. Finally, the tenth sample read at 39 foot pounds. She recorded that.

She'd tested not just five harnesses, as the rule required, but ten. Five tested at more than 30 pounds, and she recorded those readings. Five tested below 30, and she ignored them.

This was unlike any sampling or testing system I'd ever seen. I struck up a conversation with her. She showed me her log. As I'd suspected, all the readings were over 30 foot pounds. I pointed to the four samples she'd tested and ignored.

"What about those?" I asked.

"What about them?" she echoed.

"Well, you tested them, but didn't write down the readings."

"Not supposed to."

"Why?"

" 'Cause they're flukes."

"Flukes?"

"Yeah. Flukes. They tested out below 30, so they're flukes. We don't write down flukes. Boss said not to."

"But here's the thing," I said. "If you don't write down those flukes, it makes it look like all the harnesses are strong enough. But some of them aren't."

"I know that. I'm just doing what the boss said to."

I shook my head. "But what if—just suppose one of those flukes gets installed on an airplane engine?"

"Well, I wondered about that," she said. "I asked the boss. He said not to worry about it. Because I'm catching the flukes, see? I caught 'em and threw 'em down right over there."

"Uh-huh," I said faintly.

"Good thing I'm catching the flukes, huh?" she beamed.

Obviously, the sampling approach was terrible. But there's a quality image angle to this story, too. The root cause of a poor quality image goes much deeper than bad advertising or poor intrinsic quality. The root cause of a poor quality image is, ultimately, *management inconsistency toward quality*—"quality when convenient," in other words.

Examples of this attitude abound in stagnant companies:

"Better to ship a few defectives than miss a delivery date."

"Don't worry about those bad ones. Put them in the bottom of the box so the customer doesn't notice right away."

"So what if they're banged up? We"ll fill export orders with them. That way, they'll never come back."

"Look, the customer wants it today, so get it out the door. Let the field service people worry about the problems; that's what they get paid for."

"Here's how to handle it. Wait till the last minute to ship. The customer is so hard up, they'll take it, defects and all."

The workers catch on fast. It takes a nanosecond, at most, for them to get the message: Management doesn't, for all its memos and posters and rallies, *really* care about quality.

Workers react much as you'd expect. They feel contempt for management's hypocrisy and cynicism about their jobs and the organization. An atmosphere of contempt and cynicism does not breed a good quality image.

In this atmosphere, workers seldom go that extra mile. They begin to view the customer as an irritant, an object of contempt. Their service level varies, with the noisiest customer getting the best treatment. They give less than their best when they can get away with it. They say "no" because it's more convenient than saying "yes."

Cynical, negative feelings become cynical, negative actions. Such actions obviously include being indifferent to intrinsic quality—"Why should I care if no one else does?" But, even more damaging, the actions extend to aspects of the business far beyond intrinsic quality, actions that are noted and remembered by customers and prospects alike:

- The receptionist keeps a caller on hold for 15 minutes, then misroutes the call.
- The warranty claims representative deals with problems in a defensive and hostile way.
- The personnel staffer is condescending and rude to job applicants. (Job applicants buy things too!)
- The disgruntled employee tells real or imagined horror stories about the business to others.
- The advertising representative gives the media a pain in the neck by continually missing deadlines and delivering inaccurate mechanicals. (A particularly lethal mistake. Never antagonize anyone who buys ink by the barrel!)

- The credit/collections person badgers every past-due account the same way, whether it's 10 or 120 days old.
- The driver of the company-owned vehicle (with the company logo emblazoned proudly on it) drives recklessly.

Such activities counteract the intrinsic quality of your product or service. They counteract your efforts to create a good image in your advertising. All by themselves, they create a poor quality image, a hidden yet powerful enemy within your organization.

Stagnant firms overlook this. They focus on advertising—spending ever-increasing sums to counteract the poor quality image that they're creating themselves. They focus on intrinsic quality, little understanding that intrinsic quality means nothing without a strong, healthy quality image.

How do Quality Age firms build and nurture their good quality image?

Management's Responsibilities

Throughout this book, I'll stress management's vital role in the improvement process. There's no escaping the fact that the firm *is* the management. Management's beliefs, activities, and style are emulated throughout the organization. In essence, the firm's quality image is a direct reflection of management's quality image.

Here's how Quality Age management builds a good quality image:

- *Management is consistent about quality.* This may seem obvious, but management inconsistency is practically a universal failing among stagnant firms. Management must allow no deviation from the firm's quality goals, can tolerate no threat to the firm's quality image, and must set a sterling example for the work force.
- *Management views each job function in light of its impact on the quality image.* It's no longer enough to create job descriptions that specify simply duties, responsibilities, and objectives. Each function has some effect on the firm's

quality image, either directly or indirectly; job descriptions must recognize that effect and make individuals responsible for top performance.

- *Management holds workers accountable for their performance's impact on the quality image.* Having defined what effect each function has on the firm's quality image and incorporated that definition into job descriptions and the like, management must close the loop. During performance reviews, management must give worker performance against quality image goals as much weight as performance against the other goals.

- *Management includes the quality image as a factor in all strategic decisions.* In planning, management always evalutes the impact certain moves will have on factors such as sales, market share, competitive position, and the like. It's just as important for management to evaluate moves in light of the quality image. "Will this move improve our quality image or hurt it?"

A New Quality Control Department

It's hard to believe, but true: up to about 25 years ago, few firms had such a thing as a quality control department. Now, especially in manufacturing, such departments have become the norm. Their function is to monitor the intrinsic quality of the product or service.

Given the importance of a good quality image in today's Quality Age, I consider it essential for each firm to create a new quality control department: an autonomous group that is responsible for the firm's quality image. The head of this group must, in my opinion, be a key member of top management, with the authority to deal with all functions and levels of the firm. The activities of this new quality control department should include:

- *Monitoring the quality image.* In all business activities, we can't be sure we're improving until we know where we are. A major task of the new group should be to monitor the quality image on an ongoing basis. This can be done through scientifically designed surveys of current customers, past customers, and demographically selected prospects. The group should analyze the responses and provide ongoing reports to management.

- *Soliciting suggestions from workers about ways to improve the firm's quality image.* Suggestion boxes and other similar programs are all the rage today, but they tend to be passive activities (we'll discuss that later), and they tend to deal only with "hard" issues such as intrinsic quality and productivity. I recommend that the new quality control department aggressively solicit specific suggestions not just about ways to improve intrinsic quality and productivity but about ways to improve quality image as well. Along with management's new attention to the issue, this approach will raise quality image consciousness in all sectors of the work force.

- *Developing ways to improve quality image; recommending them to management.* From analyses of outside surveys and the internal suggestion program, the new quality control department should devise specific activities designed to improve the firm's quality image and recommend them to top management.

- *Using scientific scorekeeping methods to monitor the quality image.* Traditional quality control departments maintain some form of records of their activity. A quality control department that focuses on quality image must also use scorekeeping methods and analyses that are scientific and meaningful. We'll talk about some of these later in the book.

Integrated Quality Management most certainly deals with ways to improve the intrinsic quality of your product and service. But that's not enough; as Ford and other Quality Age companies have proven, a strong, positive quality image is just as important. It is, in fact, an absolute requirement in today's Quality Age.

Myth 2: The Cost of Quality Is the Amount Directly Spent to Prevent or Remedy Customer Dissatisfaction

Several years ago, at the beginning of my consulting relationship with a Fortune 100 firm, some top managers quoted the company's "cost of quality" for the previous year: $9,416,712.92.

I asked what this figure included, and they told me it was their cost to scrap totally defective products, correct defects in less-flawed products, handle customer complaints, and correct problems in the field. That $9,416,712.92 (not .91 or .93) was, in essence, what my clients considered their "cost of quality," the amount they spent to prevent customer dissatisfaction or to correct it.

They were very proud of their ability to determine this figure so specifically, and they got no argument from me there. But they also prided themselves on its small size as a percentage of their annual sales, which is where I had a serious problem.

Such thinking is common among today's stagnant firms (of which this particular client is no longer one). They add up the cost of scrap, rework, and warranty, and to them *that* is their "cost of quality." It's not even the tip of the iceberg!

The Not-So-Silent Salesman

Everything had gone fine that morning until I attempted to shave. I had arrived in Iowa the night before, scheduled to deliver a major talk to the American Society for Quality Control that morning. I always allow myself plenty of time to get ready, so I got up early. I showered, laid out my clothes, prepared to shave, and ran into a problem.

I'd bought a new can of shaving cream for this trip. I'd never used it before. And it looked as though I wouldn't be using it his morning, either. I shook it, pressed the button, and got only a weak trickle of pale liquid. No cream.

I shook the thing hard and tried again. Nothing. I really shook it hard, banged it on the counter. No cream. Nothing. Time was running short, so I made my own ersatz shaving cream from hand-soap lather and shaved my face as best I could. As you might imagine, I got more that just a close shave. I got a collection of nicks and scratches that you wouldn't believe. I daubed those with tissue as best I could, finished dressing, and then left for my talk. And I took along the shaving cream can.

My hosts greeted me warmly in the lecture hall. They couldn't help but notice the nicks and scratches on my face, and they were obviously curious about it but were polite enough not to ask—which doesn't mean I refrained from telling them about it.

I began my talk by telling the audience that my subject was quality, and I would start with an excellent example. I held up the shaving cream can for all to see. I told the group what had happened that morning. I told them that not only would I never buy that shaving cream again, but I would never buy anything that firm made again.

Further, I used that very same shaving cream can and that very same example in every lecture and seminar I gave from then on. I figure I passed the word about that brand of shaving cream to over 10,000 people. I'd still be using it today—except that the shaving cream maker has become my client!

Unlike stagnant firms, which figure that their cost of poor quality includes only scrap, rework, warranty—what they spend to prevent or remedy customer dissatisfaction—Quality Age firms recognize several "hidden" costs of poor quality–costs that make scrap, rework and warranty pale by comparison.

The first hidden cost is the *cost of lost business*. I was serious when I told my audience that I'd never buy that shaving cream again. So its maker lost my business. Further, I never bought anything else made by that firm: more lost business. What does all that add up to in a year? Or five years? Multiply that figure by the number of other customers just like me, across the contry and around the world, who had the same experience. What cost are we talking about now?

Then there's bad word of mouth. I personally told some 10,000 people about my experience with that shaving cream. How many of them refrained from buying that product, based on my experience? Sure, I was in a unique position to communicate my experience. I even used the defective can as a not-so-silent salesman. But all customers have the power to communicate the bad news—and they use it. According to a study, the average disgruntled customer passes his or her experience along to 22 other people. Bad news, unfortunately, travels much faster than good.

The second of the hidden costs of poor quality is *added marketing expense*. In order to maintain market share and grow, we have to replace our lost customers. This costs money for more TV ads, more promotions. The third of the hidden costs of poor quality is *cost to repair our quality image*. This is an especially painful cost since it's spent to repair the damage we caused ourselves.

When you think about these three costs, you can see how truly expensive a poor quality image is. We can never calculate that expense the way we can calculate the expense of scrap, rework, and warranty; but these three hidden costs of poor quality are definitely real.

Many stagnant firms don't even acknowledge that these costs exist, let alone take steps to control them. Quality Age management, on the other hand, recognizes that mistakes, defects, and lapses in the quality image don't come free. They cost everyone: they're money out of everyone's pockets.

Myth 3: Quality Is Meeting
Customer Requirements

Right now, you're probably shaking your head: "That's a *myth?*" Yes, it is—at least the way it's practiced today. I think that the concept of meeting customer "requirements" has driven more firms into stagnation than any other cause.

Here's how the cycle works: The firm begins as an entrepreneurship. It has an angle, a hook, a dynamic business idea. It also has precious few resources in its early days and lives with the wolf at the door. Because of this, and thanks to its small size, it maintains the closest of relationships with its customers. It values and prizes and loves its customers. It can't afford to lose even one, so it quite naturally takes great pains to accommodate them, learn specifically what they want, and deliver on it.

With success comes growth, and growth brings an array of problems:

- *Growth brings prosperity.* That's a problem, you say? It certainly can be. Without the wolf at the door, the need to know what the customers want seems not to be as immediate or urgent as it was before.

- *Growth generates a larger, more varied audience of customers and prospects.* This large variety makes it more difficult to get a handle on what customers really want. Instead of dealing with individual trees, we're dealing with a forest.

- *Growth increases the size of the firm.* As a struggling entrepreneurship, the firm consisted of a small group of people with intimate ties and blurred lines of responsibility. Everyone knew what each customer wanted; everyone knew what everyone else was doing; everyone worked together to deliver that. Growth stretches those intimate ties and eventually breaks them. Departments and power centers spring up. Lines of communication become irregular. Overall, translating "what the customers want" into meaningful change within the firm becomes harder and harder to do.

- *Growth increases arrogance on the part of management.* The attitude often becomes, "We must be doing something right; why change it?" Management loses its immediate, personal interest in keeping up with what the customers want. They stop questioning customers; even worse, they stop questioning themselves.

With size comes bureaucracy: staff people and departments, insulated from the front lines, who, in the interest of efficiency, begin to standardize. Over time, they create an elaborate network of plans, policies, and specifications that govern how the product or service is made and delivered.

Standardization is not bad, in and of itself. The demands of volume require it. What hurts the firm is the insidious way that network of standards comes to replace hard knowledge of what the customer wants and expects today. Inevitably, the firm begins to pay more attention to its own standards—its self-created view of what its customers want. And the term that is most often used for this self-created view is *customer requirements*.

The firm's mission changes. Instead of a commitment to deliver "what the customer wants or expects," it strives to "meet customer requirements." The firm measures its performance against those "customer requirements." This change in mission inevitably has three negative effects: The company loses touch with customer expectations, loses sight of priorities, and lets the status quo triumph.

Losing Touch with Customer Expectations

Time, of course, moves along; what customers want, need, and expect changes. But the firm that "meets customer requirements" tends not to change with the passage of time. The variance between the firm's products or services and what the customers want at any given point grows wider and wider.

Losing Sight of Priorities

A firm like this tends to treat all its plans, policies, and specifications as equally important. Having engraved all these in stone, it seldom reappraises them in light of the current situation. It tends to enforce even the most trivial policy or specification, regardless of the cost, even if its impact on the achievement of customer expectations is nil.

One household products firm, for example, regulated the radius of the spray emitted by a can of aerosol to within $1/5000$ of an inch. It was extremely costly to enforce this specification, yet the firm went on doing it. Had this "customer requirement" not been engraved in stone, someone at the firm would have looked at the specification and asked the logical question: "Why are we doing this? Does a customer really care if the spray radius varies by $5/1000$ or $7/1000$ of an inch?"

Letting the Status Quo Triumph

The firm that "meets customer requirements" tends to become satisfied with this goal, even proud of it. In fact, "meeting customer requirements" becomes an alibi, rather than a goal. The firm loses the habit of questioning what it is doing and seeking ways to improve.

Within the firm, various process stages begin to focus on their own individual goals and lose sight of the ultimate function and purpose of the product or the service. Within the process stages, individual workers become accustomed to "hitting the number," doing the minimum that is expected of them, and that's all. The result is a firm that prides itself on "meeting customer requirements" that have, due to forces of change, become inconsistent with customer expectations.

A firm like this is operating at ever-increasing isolation from its customers. It is composed of groups and individuals with no incentive to improve. It is a firm in stagnation.

Such a stagnant firm is, as we've seen in the past 20 years, extremely vulnerable to competition. To compete and take market share, a competitor doesn't have to be *tremendously* better, only a little better. In Olympic sprint competitions, the victor may win by only .001 of a second and still be the victor.

The firm that is "meeting customer requirements" leaves windows of opportunity open to a potential competitor. All the competitor has to do is deliver *what the customer wants and expects today*. The stagnant firm, self-satisfied that it is "meeting customer requirements," suddenly loses market share and has no idea what happened.

In the Quality Age, then, quality is not "meeting customer requirements." Quality is much tougher than that. Quality is delivering products and services that, in every respect, are equal to or better than what the customer *wants* and *expects* (not just "requires") today.

"Meeting customer requirements" is an internal term coined by stagnant firms. Quality Age firms, on the other hand, define quality in *external* terms — in terms of the customers' *current* needs and wants: not just what they wanted last year, or what management says they want.

Quality isn't what we say it is. It is, ultimately, what our customers think it is. Conceptually, quality is *a favorable relationship between what customers expect to receive and their perception of the value of what they receive.*

Quality is, in essence, a positive and unique mix of perception, performance, and price.

Perception is especially important because it works two ways. First, there is the customer's perception of your firm, which we call the Quality Image. Next down the ladder is the customers' perception of what they will receive from you, a perception that you play an important role in developing through advertising and other communication. Third is the perception of value, which is a relationship between *price* and *performance.*

Given all that, there's no way to distill a more specific definition of quality that applies to all products and services. There is, in fact, a specific and complex quality definition for every single product and service. This definition combines *intrinsic* characteristics with *conceptual* characteristics. For the sake of convenience, I'll call this definition of quality the *customer goal.*

The customer goal is not only specific, detailed, and complex, it's also constantly changing. What you adhered to last year may not have been on target to begin with and is certainly outmoded in some respects by now.

Here's a relatively simple example of how complex a customer goal can be and how it can change.

The Automated Teller Machine (ATM). How does the customer define quality in ATM service? What, specifically, is the customer goal? We could say "functionality and durability at a fair price." But when you apply that to an ATM, it doesn't say much, does it? When you ask the customer, the definition can get very specific. The customer wants an ATM that is available when he or she needs it. Specifically, it should be open 24 hours a day, because people's schedules vary so much. This also means that the machines should not break down very much.

The customer wants an ATM that is secure. Specifically, the programming should be designed to prevent unauthorized access. In addition, the physical location of the machine is a factor. It should be well lighted and in a public place so that the customer doesn't have to fear being mugged.

The customer wants an ATM that allows a variety of transactions. Here, the factor of time comes into play. Today the bank may offer checking, savings, and credit card services. If, next month, the bank begins to provide signature-secured lines of credit, the customer will expect access to them through the ATM as well. The bank must change accordingly.

Quality, then, is what the customers want and expect today. Quality is specific to the product or service right now. Quality is delivering consistently on the customer goal.

How do Quality Age firms determine what the customer goal is?

First Step: Listen. Customers provide feedback constantly. Comments, letters, suggestions, warranty activity, competitive forces, and trade publications are all channels of feedback that Quality Age firms analyze in order to get hard facts on the customer goal.

Quality Age management stresses to every member of the organization the *feedback on the customer goal* is welcome, even rewarded. While employee suggestion programs are widely used, there are other techniques as well.

Second Step: Research. Listening, while essential, is also passive. Information obtained in this way tends to reflect the current situation; the competitive edge comes from discovering future trends and acting upon them before anyone else does.

Quality Age firms engage in active, ongoing *research*: not one-shot inquiries, but a formalized program. The techniques I recommend are the same as those used to monitor your quality image — scientific surveys of present and past customers, surveys of demographically selected prospects, focus groups.

The questions go from the general to the specific: What do you like about our product or service? What do you dislike? Why did you buy from us? Why not? What would make you buy again? What can we do to make it better? *Specifically?*

In addition to surveying these groups about your own performance, question them about competitors' performance too. How are they better than you? How are they worse?

Third Step: Scorekeeping. Obtaining the data is the first step; analyzing the data through scientific scorekeeping methods is what makes the date useful to Quality Age firms. This is particularly vital in instances where customers themselves can't express what they want. The top firms learn to "read between the lines," perform tests and sophisticated analyses. We'll talk about some of the scorekeeping methods later in the book.

From these research and analysis activities, each Quality Age firm develops a living, breathing customer goal—an objective that is real.

Myth 4: Quality and Productivity Are Antithetical

From the dawn of the Industrial Age—if not the dawn of time—productivity has been the American way. We grew up believing that bigger is always better. Crank it up. Get 'em out the door. Pedal to the metal. More, more, more!

This tendency continues today, well after the dawn of the Quality Age. The stagnant firms see quality as a convenience in some sense, acceptable as long as it does not interfere with productivity: "Quality? Neat idea. Tell you what. You can have all the quality you want. Just don't mess with productivity."

They seem to think that quality and productivity are mutually exclusive, that you can have quality, or productivity, but not both. Quality up, the stagnant thinking goes, equals productivity down—and vice versa.

Quality Age firms have learned that quality cannot be subordinate to productivity. But productivity can't be subordinate to quality, either. Here's an illustration, about my own company for a change.

We began our business by providing consulting and training services in an improvement tool called Statistical Process Control (about which you'll learn more about later). SPC uses statistics: easy statistics, but lots of them. The work can get very boring.

Perfect for a computer, right? I thought so. What's more, there were no SPC software packages on the market, not a single one. It was a golden opportunity.

I knew very little about programming, but I had a friend who did. Dave is an old classmate from my Chicago days. A bona fide genius and a brilliant software design engineer. I hired him to come to Detroit and design an SPC software package for us.

Well, he came and sat down with me. I went over all the SPC functions with him. I showed him how the calculations worked, how the charting should be done. He had no problems learning the concepts. They're really pretty simple. We agreed on the basic features of the program. Then he went to work.

Days went by, then weeks. Pretty soon, it was months.

Dave worked like a demon, but things went slowly. Whenever I checked with him, he'd made progress, but nothing was ever quite good enough for him. Everything always needed "just a little more work." He tinkered and polished, fussed and massaged, niggled and fine-tuned.

I'm as patient as the next person, and I don't like to interfere with an expert. But this project was turning into a black hole. Finally, I asked him to run the program for me. I had to see what it looked like.

It wouldn't even boot.

But Dave wasn't concerned about that. He had been spending hours and hours designing the sign-on logo screen. And despite his hours of effort, he *still* wasn't satisfied with it!

I took him off the project and brought in a new programmer. He looked at what Dave had done so far and decided to start over. Eventually he completed On-Line Analyst, our SPC software package.

It has sold well. But I'll always feel a little disappointed. For by the time it came out, a handful of other SPC software packages had hit the market. We'd missed our golden opportunity.

I know Dave's a genius. I'm sure his version of the program would have been wonderful—had he ever finished it. But I don't think he ever would have. This was a case of quality run amok. It shows clearly that productivity has to be there, too. Without it, nothing gets done. Ernest Hemingway, talking about writing, summed it up perfectly. "You never finish a book. You abandon it."

There are environments where such an obsession with quality is positive. Medieval monks, who each spent a lifetime illuminating 20 pages of manuscript, come to mind. But in twentieth-century American business, productivity will always be vital. The question is, how does it fit with quality?

In today's stagnant firms, quality and productivity don't work together at all. This is evident in the very structure of such firms. Where quality is recognized as a factor at all, it's treated separately from productivity. There are two competing efforts: a quality group on one side, working toward a goal; a productivity group on the other, working toward another goal, like a football team which commits to a running game one week and a passing game the next.

The result is factionalism: quality people versus productivity people; a police-state atmosphere. You can't get much more anti-improvement than that!

A New Attitude

The reason stagnant firms view productivity and quality as antithetical is that they're viewing the issue from their own point of view rather than from their customers' point of view. Quality Age firms view quality and productivity *from the point of view of their customers' interests*. They're constantly asking: What is quality to our customer? What does our customer want?

Earlier, we defined quality as a positive relationship between what customers expect to receive and their perception of the value of what they received—a positive mix of perception, performance and *price*.

Performance is on one side of the balance; price is on the other. The customer compares the performance (perceived if not actual) of our product or service with the price we're charging for it. What we charge affects the customer's desire for the product; it also colors the customer's perception of the product and of our firm.

Customers instinctively make a *value judgement*. A price that is too high may cost us business because customers think we're trying to fleece them. More commonly, too high a price costs us business because customers turn to a competitor offering what they perceive as a better value.

Value is the key word. Value judgments are nebulous things; predicting what will be perceived as a value is definitely an inexact science. Of course, we can provide the best value simply by setting prices far below everyone else—but in most cases that would mean losing money, which would put us out of business.

The key to pricing, which gives us profits and is perceived as the best value by the customer, is *productivity*—the most efficient use of our time, energy, and resources.

Since a value price is part of quality, and productivity is what enables us to offer a value price, productivity is, then, not the antithesis of quality, but a *subset* of it. That's how Quality Age firms look at it.

How, then, do we deal with those competing entities within our businesses: quality forces and productivity forces at each other's throats? How do we eliminate this negative competition without inflicting an economics course on our people?

The answer to the problem lies in revising the ways we measure quality and productivity. Today, most of us measure them separately. That's the essence of negative competition. We must now measure them together.

This may strike you as impossible, but I assure you it isn't. I've created such a measurement system called the Quality/Productivity Index. It's the most powerful tool I know of to make quality and productivity truly synergistic. When work is measured by this simple index, amazing things start to happen. Factionalism fades. Wrangling over competing objectives goes away. People work together toward a single goal. Productivity improves, and quality improves along with it. We'll explore how this index works in Chapter 7.

In this chapter, we've identified and dealt with four quality myths—myths that separate stagnant firms from Quality Age firms.

- *Quality is more than a technically perfect product or service;* just as important, if not more so, is a strong, healthy quality image.

- *The cost of quality* is more than the amount directly spent to prevent or remedy customer dissatisfaction; it also includes the cost of lost and referral business—a staggering sum.

- *Quality is not "meeting customer requirements";* it is delivering consistently against a detailed, timely customer goal.

- *Quality and productivity are not antithetical;* productivity is, in fact, a subset of quality.

Quality Age firms embrace those realities. And they've done much more. Having identified the dynamic customer goal, they've reoriented their processes—the means by which they produce and deliver products and services—to deliver on that customer goal consistently.

Stagnant firms are a different story. Their grasp of the prevailing customer goal is vague, and their processes are afflicted with malaise that prevents them from delivering consistently high-quality products and services.

How do Quality Age firms maintain dynamism within their processes? How can stagnant firms replace malaise with the dynamism and vitality it takes to deliver quality consistently?

2

Up from Stagnation: Reviving the Entrepreneurial Spirit

In today's hot, competitive marketplace, where products and services come and go so fast you'll miss them if you blink, it's indeed astounding to look at the record of the Model T Ford. The first Model T appeared in 1908; the last one came off the line in 1927. During those 19 years, Ford built about 15 million of them.

The tough, unpretentious little car was a legend in its own time. Songs were written and sung about it. Jokes—complimentary ones—were told about it. Competitions were conducted in which Model Ts race cross-country, climbed mountains, and more. Fifteen million Model T Fords gave their maker an unprecedented 57 percent share of the U.S. auto marketplace.

But these 15 million Model T Fords were all, thanks to the adamance of Henry Ford, virtually alike. And that in the end was their undoing. In the early 1920s, the Model T began to suffer in comparison with other cars. Ford's market share began to erode; sales declined; the jokes became unkind. The Model T's shortcomings did not go unnoticed within the company. Ford designers, executives, and dealers pleaded for enhancements and improvements to the car and/or the development of an entirely new model to counter the challenge of hard chargers like Chevrolet.

At first, Henry Ford waved off the pleas blithely. "The only thing wrong with the Model T," he said, "is that we can't make them fast enough."[5] By 1926, however, even the founder recognized the threat. But even so he furiously rejected any proposal to improve the car itself. Instead, he dictated changes in the marketing program designed to bolster sales: a price cut and an expansion in the dealer network.

Neither move had a positive effect on the Model T's flagging fortunes. Finally, the old genius threw in the towel and plunged into the development of the Model A, which appeared the following year.

The Model A was a sales phenomenon in its own right. On its first day in Ford showrooms, some 50,000 orders were taken for it in New York City alone. But, in his heart, Henry Ford never accepted the forces of change that made it necessary to discontinue the Model T. "The only thing wrong with that car," he groused many years later, "was that people stopped buying it."[6]

The Decline of Entrepreneurship

The Model T story illustrates a business cycle that has been repeated, with variations, down through the years and is very much evident in the Quality Age. What started every single one of today's giant businesses? An entrepreneur. What built them to dominance? The entrepreneurial spirit. Then one of two things happened. Those firms that were able to renew and sustain the entrepreneurial spirit evolved into Quality Age companies. Those that did not do so sank into stagnation.

What are the characteristics of the entrepreneur and, by extension, the entrepreneurial spirit? The dictionary defines an *entrepreneur* as "one who organizes and directs a business undertaking, assuming the risk for the sake of the profit." This definition says nothing about personality traits, but those are definitive too. Here are some of the characteristics that make an entrepreneur:

1. *The willingness to take risks.* The entrepreneur is very much a risk-taker, an independent thinker, a defier of convention. The entrepreneur is partly a creator, partly an assimilator, one who looks at things differently from everyone else and finds value in ideas.

   Henry Ford, for example, became obsessed with mechanics and engineering at an early age. Though raised in a farming environment, he defied the life envisioned for him to pursue his dream. He marched to a different drummer his entire life.

2. *An unshakeable belief in the validity of a unique customer goal.* The entrepreneur has a unique perception of a customer goal, seeing a need that no one else believes is practical. In Ford's time, cars were luxuries, designed and built for the moneyed class. Ford, a man of humble origins, was intimately aware of the needs and wants of the people around him. He believed that they wanted and needed automobiles as much if not more than the upper classes, and he felt very strongly that they should have them.

   It was an altruistic vision to be sure, but it had a more practical side. Just as Willie Sutton robbed banks because "that's where the money is," Ford produced practical, affordable cars for average people because there were a lot more of them than anyone else.

3. *Determination.* Called "single-minded and persevering" by supporters and "a fanatic" by detractors, the entrepreneur does not waver in the pursuit of the customer goal.

   Henry Ford was commonly referred to as Crazy Henry. Yet he endured business setbacks and the betrayal of backers without ever once taking his eyes off the customer goal of a practical, economical, reliable car.

4. *Close contact with the process.* We've already said that the entrepreneur has an intimate awareness of customer needs. Similarly, the entrepreneur is intimately aware of the abilities and workings of every aspect of the process that produces the product or service. He or she is close to the designers, to the people who actually make the

product or execute the service, to those who advertise it, market it, and sell it. This intimacy, combined with the entrepreneur's inherent authority, gives the firm tremendous flexibility.

The entrepreneur keeps tabs on everything, making sure that every function of the firm contributes to the customer goal. As things change, the entrepreneur can implement changes to the firm's workings with blinding speed. Henry Ford, at heart an engineer, loved to stroll the production lines; but he was also a visible presence in the design rooms and among the dealers in the field.

5. *Mistrust of bureaucracy.* Simplicity is a key secret of the successful entrepreneur. Therefore, most successful entrepreneurs resist the inherent complications of growth. While on the one hand they strive for growth with all their might, on the other hand they systematically inhibit the development of departments, rules, procedures, and bureaucracy. They view such things as interferences that distract the organization from delivering on the customer goal.

Few entrepreneurs hated bureaucracy as much as Henry Ford. For many years, his only corporate title was "Mister." No matter how large the firm got, he insisted on knowing everything that was going on, even to the point of employing a company spy network. His hatred of paperwork was legendary; once, in the early days, he demonstrated to an accounting clerk the "proper" way to handle a backlog of correspondence: pitch it out the window.

6. *Unquenchable thirst for improvement.* Entrepreneurs inevitably begin with what they view as a "better idea." They see what they're doing as an improvement over what existed before, and they seem never to lose the appetite for improvement.

Entrepreneurs maintain intimate contact with the customer goal on the one hand and with all functions of the firm on the other; they strip away clutter, prioritize resources, and focus all energies on *improvement*—making the product, or furnishing the service, better and better.

This trait sets a strong example for the rest of the firm. The thirst for improvement becomes contagious and self-sustaining. In addition to being a masterful engineer, Henry Ford was a master at inspiring his workers to excel. In the early years of the Model T, his goal was to produce a car a minute. Though this level of productivity was unheard of, Ford achieved it. Ford was not content to rest on this achievement, though. By the end of the Model T's run, Ford was producing one *every 10 seconds.*

The common thread among these entrepreneurial traits is *communication:*

- *Communication with customers;* determining the customer goal and continuing to learn about it as it changes.
- *Communication among functions.* Rather than being above the various functions of the firm, the entrepreneur is *central* to them. He or she is their nexus. The entrepreneur knows what the problems are, knows what the issues are, and can cause the firm to react to changes at literally a moment's notice.

Unfortunately, the classic entrepreneurship seems to have a limited shelf-life. The Model T episode is a case in point. There, another classic entrepreneurial trait—intransigence—was his undoing.

Initially, the car matched the prevailing customer goal perfectly. Like all cars, it was better transportation than the horse. Like some cars, it was very durable. Like no other car of its time, it was within the economic reach of masses of people. Model Ts sold faster than Ford could make them, even back in the days when there were few decent roads to drive them on!

But over the years the customer goal changed, prompted by engineering advances made by General Motors. People wanted the convenience and safety of self-starting engines. They wanted the safety of hydraulic brakes. They wanted the comfort of advanced suspension systems. As roads improved, they wanted the better power and speed produced by six- and eight-cylinder engines. As cars became expressions of personal values and taste, people wanted choices in styles and colors.

Thanks to the stubbornness of Henry Ford, his company did not change its product to match the changing customer goal—not until its back was to the wall. And it never regained the awesome pre-eminence, it had once had; strong competitor though the Model A was, Ford's market share dropped to some 34 percent and hovered there from then on.

Ford was still respectable, but no longer dominant—all because of its failure to adjust, adapt, and deliver what the customers wanted. Henry Ford certainly had the power to do that; he simply chose not to.

Though such intransigence is atypical, the loss of the entrepreneurial spirit is, unfortunately, quite common.

The Stagnation Cycle

Every single one of today's stagnant firms began as an entrepreneurship, with the qualities that I have outlined in the previous section.

Today, they are ailing, unwieldy giants. What happened in between? Generally, the first thing that happens is that the entrepreneur loses a *central* role in the firm. Sometimes this happens because the entrepreneur simply leaves, voluntarily or involuntarily. Many entrepreneurs are excellent "idea" people, in love with the creative process, but are bored and frustrated by the challenges of managing growth.

In any event, the entrepreneur is eventually succeeded by professional business managers. These people typically bring with them business experience and abilities that the entrepreneur may have lacked. Unfortunately, the seeds of stagnation can be sown at this point for, too often, these managers lack *the entrepreneur's passion for the product or service* and the passion for delivering what the customer wants.

Many managers replace this passion with self-established secondary goals—sales growth, productivity, the bottom line—superseding the entrepreneur's goal of giving customers what they want.

Then, as volume builds and the firm increases in size, "organization" sets in. Functions such as design, service or manufacturing, sales and marketing—all of which once merged in the entrepreneur—become discrete. They become entities in their own right, with their own languages and their own goals.

What was once a lean, flexible process, producing the product or service in a series of steps, becomes rigid and unwieldy. Each step in the process is performed in isolation. Each step works toward some sort of target or goal, whose relationship with the overall purpose, the customer goal, becomes vague and, at best, secondary.

Even worse, the work performed at each step begins to vary from one time to the next. This variation gives rise to quality problems—things that don't work, break, taste bad, and don't get delivered on time.

Just as the entrepreneurial spirit is characterized by communication, the onset of stagnation is characterized by *lack of communication*. The firm no longer receives the communications of its customers. The functions, having grown apart, speak their own languages, like the nations of Europe. The process steps, isolated from each other and from intimate awareness of the customer goal, do their work blindly.

All management knows is that the firm is having "quality problems." How does the stagnant firm react?

The Final Nail

The entrepreneur was the nexus between the process on the one hand and customer expectations on the other. He or she made constant and almost subconscious adjustments to ensure that the former satisfied the latter.

When entrepreneurship is replaced by stagnation, the firm no longer works to satisfy customers. Instead, it settles for meeting its own "specs" or "customer requirements." Its goal is now to keep customers from complaining, and the usual strategy for doing that is a band-aid approach to quality called *final inspection*.

The theory, as expressed in the spark plug commercial I talked about earlier, is that the firm's work is inspected for errors and defects before being sent to customers. This inspection is done against some sort of standard, usually defined in isolation. Products or services that meet the standard go on to the customer. Those that don't are corrected or discarded.

In theory, this is "quality." But the realities are these:

- Inspection does not improve anything because it detects only symptoms, not causes.
- Inspection is defensive. Its real purpose is to keep customers from complaining, not to create customers who brag.
- Inspection standards tend to be flexible. Products that would fail inspection during slow demand periods magically pass inspection when demand is heavy.
- Because inspection takes place after the work is done, it is in fact an admission that the process cannot consistently produce quality.
- Inspection is the most wasteful activity in business today.

Why do I say that?

Inspection Is Inefficient

I'm willing to admit that in theory inspection would be an acceptable measure if it caught 100 percent of the defects. But it doesn't. Most firms can't inspect every single aspect of every single unit of output; they must settle for inspecting *samples*, which by definition allows some amount of subquality products or services to slip through.

And even those firms with low enough volume to be able to inspect every single aspect of every single product or service can't possibly catch all the defects. It has been tested and proven, time and again, that even 200 percent, 300 percent inspection fails to catch everything.

Inspection Is All Expense and No Gain

What does inspection really tell you? If inspection finds defects, it tells you only how much waste and loss you've incurred. It tells you little if anything about the *causes* of those defects; it contributes nothing to the effort to correct those causes. If, on the other hand, inspection finds *no* defects, then it has been wholly useless!

Inspection Discourages a Quality Attitude

You can talk quality all you want to the workers within the process, but as long as inspection is the principal form of quality control, the workers will not take quality totally to heart. Inspection is ultimately a placebo, a fictitious safety net. It absolves the people within the process—who have the knowledge and the ability (not necessarily the authority) to act—from responsibility for quality.

Inspection places responsibility for quality upon people at the end of the process, people who are extraneous to the process and unfamiliar with it. These people—the inspectors—lack the authority, the responsibility, and the knowledge to act.

Inspection is nonsensical, yet stagnant firms hang onto it for dear life partly because "we've always done it this way" and, more critically, because they have no idea how to bring quality into their processes. We can't do away with inspection completely till we have fully implemented the principles of Integrated Quality Management. But then, in most cases, we can eliminate it.

A Grim Picture

Failure to deliver on the customer goal cost Ford Motor company its dominant role 60 years ago, and that same failure is a leading cause of stagnation in many of today's firms—but it's by no means the only cause.

In sum, the cause is the utter loss of the entrepreneurial spirit that gave the firm its start. The stagnant firm's process has become encrusted with rigidity and past practice. Each step within the process acts in isolation from the rest, working toward some specious goal, which, like government spending programs, develops a life of its own. It becomes self-justifying. No one ever wants to do better.

Then, at the end, the expensive and inefficient inspection step sorts things out. "Acceptable" products or services go on to customers. So do defective and marginal output that is either missed by inspection or waived.

You can imagine the effect all of this has on that forgotten element, the customers. They receive products or services that at best marginally meet their expectations and at worst don't function at all. The quality image goes into decline. Some customers take their business elsewhere; others stay but become watchful, hostile, more demanding.

As business declines, the stagnant firm spends even more on advertising and marketing to counteract its increasingly negative image. The stagnant firm puts increased pressure on productivity, inevitably creating more bad products faster. And the stagnant firm counteracts its decaying bottom line by cutting expenses, even when doing so hurts quality.

All these measures produce the most damaging effect of all: lack of energy and dynamism, which directly reflects worker attitudes.

- Workers see quite clearly that management's main commitment is to productivity and the bottom line, rather than customers.
- Workers witness management's inconsistency about quality.
- Workers see defective products and services going out the door, either because inspection misses them or management waives them.
- Workers offer no suggestions or ideas because management ignores them.
- Workers bear the brunt of customer dissatisfaction and, at the same time, are management's scapegoat.
- Workers wonder: "Why should I put out? What's in it for me?"

So they don't put out. They put in their hours, punch out, and go home. This is a far, far cry from the days of the entrepreneur, wouldn't you say?

Bring Back the Entrepreneur

Entrepreneurship is not dead in America. Far from it. It's alive and well in America's booming small business sector—the most dynamic in the world. Compare the United States with Europe, for example. Exact figures are impossible to obtain, but clearly the U.S. small business entrepreneur sector is far larger than that of the European Economic Community. That's a function of our free enterprise system, and—more important—of our unique characteristics as Americans.

The entrepreneurial spirit is also alive and well in the larger firms that have become Quality Age companies. It's to those firms that stagnant companies look for their examples.

There's no reason that we can't restore the entrepreneurial spirit even to huge conglomerates that have fallen into stagnation. Some say that notion is impractical. Sheer size makes it impossible, they insist. The days of old Henry Ford roaming the line, talking to workers, checking up, showing them a better way, are long gone.

In response I would point to top executives like Sam Walton of Wal-mart and Sam Johnson of Johnson Wax. They're intimately involved in their firms and their processes. Most important, they are *communicators*.

Half of communication (sometimes more than half) is listening. True managers with the entrepreneurial spirit *listen* to their customers constantly, staying abreast of the customer goal: the customers' needs, wants, and expectations in all their details.

Entrepreneurial managers *communicate* the customer goal to every facet of the firm. And they elicit feedback from their people, *listen* to it, and act upon it. And finally, entrepreneurial managers *foster communication*, close ties, a cohesive network within the organization.

There's no law that says that the entrepreneurial spirit is the exclusive property of small firms. Communication is the key. Communication has sustained the entrepreneurial spirit in, for example, Domino's Inc., despite its incredible growth. Communication helped restore the entrepreneurial spirit in the

Ford Motor Company, making possible its resurgence in the 1980s. Effective communication will restore the entrepreneurial spirit to the stagnant firms of the 1990s and keep stagnation from overtaking the rest.

How IQM Can Make It Happen

The principles of Integrated Quality Management, as utilized by today's Quality Age firms, nurture the essence of entrepreneurship—dynamism, flexibility, service to customers.

The first phase, as outlined in Chapter 1, is to *establish a system to learn and stay current on the customer goal*. The customer goal in its detailed form is always expressed in the customers' own language. Therefore, it's long on generalities and short on specifics in its raw stages. So the system must be able to find out what customers "really mean" as well as what they initially say.

To illustrate, let's say we're running a hamburger restaurant. Since 99.5 percent of Americans have probably patronized such places, this is a scenario with which you're familiar. What is the customer goal? Fast, cheap, and good, right?

Through intensified research, we can get our customers to be a little more specific than that. By "fast," they tell us they "don't want to hang around waiting." They also want the convenience of using a drive-through.

By "cheap," they're telling us they don't want to spend as much at our restaurant as they would at a more formal sit-down restaurant.

By "good," they're telling us a multitude of things. "Good" means a variety of ingredients. "Good" means methods of preparation that combine those ingredients in a way that produces pleasing tastes. "Good" means food that is nourishing and does not contribute to health disorders. "Good" also applies to the form in which the food is served; "Good" even refers to physical appearance of the food and the quality of the service that delivers it.

The second phase brings dynamism into the process as the Quality Age firm *translates the customer goal into action*. This redefines the process so that it is constantly producing prod-

ucts and services that are consistent with the prevailing customer goal. The steps that compose this phase are called *quality
function deployment* by their Quality Age adherents. Together
they form a strategy that replaces stagnation with dynamism,
creates the entrepreneurial atmosphere of communication, and
enables the process to work toward a single objective: meeting
the customer goal and ultimately transcending it.

Step 1: Translating the Components of the Customer Goal into Measurable Technical Language

The Quality Age firm always initially expresses the customer
goal in the customers' own nontechnical language. After that,
though, the goal must be converted into the firm's own particular jargon, which is often technical. It's also important to
translate the customer goal into a form that renders its components *measurable*.

For example, our hamburger restaurant customers want
"fast" service; they don't want to hang around waiting.
We might translate that requirement into an "average order
delivery time." We can then survey customers again or
perform actual tests to determine the optimal average order
wait time.

Issues such as taste are, by nature, nebulous. They don't
lend themselves well to measurement, or so you might think.
Quality Age firms get around this problem by developing arbitrary and objective rating systems. On a scale of 1 to 10, where
do your customers rate the taste of your food? What rating do
they expect?

One way or the other, each element of the customer goal
becomes a specific, measurable attribute.

Step 2: Establishing Customer Goal Targets

For each element of the customer goal, the firm establishes a
target. Quality Age firms aim nowhere but up. They always
strive to deliver on the customer goal appreciably better than
anyone else. They set their targets by assessing competitor

performance and by learning the preferences of the customers. And they always aim high.

Our hamburger restaurant may have a direct competitor who delivers orders in an average of five minutes. We learn from our customers that speed of delivery is a vital issue; we therefore set a target of four minutes.

Step 3: Pinpointing Each Function's Contribution to the Customer Goal

The *process* is the system that produces the product or service. It consists of a series of steps, and each step has a prescribed function. At this stage, the Quality Age firm looks at the function of each step in the process and identifies its effect on the firm's overall performance against the customer goal.

This is important. In stagnant firms, many functions appear to have no relationship at all between their work and customer satisfaction. But each function *must* have such a relationship.

Take our hamburger restaurant. The laborer who unloads the supply truck probably sees no relationship between what he does and customer satisfaction. But there are several relationships. If he doesn't work fast enough, the kitchen may run out of key supplies, slowing delivery of orders and causing customers to wait for their orders. If he doesn't put a fresh supply of hamburger buns in the right location, the stock may not rotate correctly and customers may receive stale hamburger buns.

Quality Age firms know that every function and step in the process has an impact on the customer goal. They constantly endeavor to determine just what that impact is and make sure the workers involved are aware of it.

Step 4: Establishing Targets for Each Process Step

Just as each element of the customer goal has a target, so must each step in the process. Quality Age firms set performance targets for each step, making sure that those targets are consistent with the customer goal.

For example, our hamburger restaurant's overall goal of a four-minute order delivery time may require the cook to produce two dozen patties every five minutes during peak demand periods. There targets must be carefully defined.

Step 5: Instituting Reduction of Variation as a Goal for Each Process Step

It's a fine thing to set all these targets. But, let's face it, we live in an imperfect world populated by human beings. All sorts of things are going to prevent us from hitting those targets consistently. To insist that targets be hit very single time and to penalize failure to do so is absurd.

Quality Age firms know that. Rather than insisting on an unreasonable standard like "perfection," they focus their efforts on controlling a real-world phenomenon: *variation*. I bring this up now because, as you'll see, variation is a key element in quality. We'll come back to it again and again as the book goes on.

Step 6: Establishing Supplier-Customer Relationships within the Process

A process is very much like a chain reaction. Each step does various things and hands the result off to the next step. The isolation between steps in today's stagnant firms is due to wide variation in performance and an element of uncertainty as to what each step is expected to receive and to deliver.

This atmosphere of uncertainty and distrust is visible everywhere in stagnant firms, where many factions find it easier to do business with outsiders than with other parts of their own organization. A certain major computer manufacturer, for example, once ordered several units of its own computer equipment from an independent, outside dealer because it was easier to do that than to requisition the same equipment from within its own firm!

Quality Age firms see to it that each function within the process stays close to the others. Employees at each process step know, at all times, what they will receive from employees at the previous step (in measurable terms) and what they are expected to deliver to the next step (in measurable terms). Further, the employees at each step regularly evaluate the work of employees at the previous step, using measurable performance ratings that are clear and easily understood by all concerned.

In the hamburger restaurant, the people who assemble the sandwiches should have confidence that they will receive fresh buns, properly cooked patties, and a consistent supply of condiments. They should also know that they are expected to deliver sandwiches that conform to order within a specified period of time.

This type of information automatically opens opportunities of necessary communication between process steps, but Quality Age firms do much more.

Step 7: Establishing Communication Venues

Here, of course, I am talking about teams and team meetings. We'll discuss how to manage teams in depth in a later chapter. Right now we'll talk about the two kinds of teams that are used by Quality Age firms.

The first kind of team is composed of people who work in a single process step. This team is responsible for the performance of a certain type of work. They have a defined, measurable target. There is a historical range of variation that they are expected to reduce. They stay aware of the impact their work has on the customer goal.

The second kind of team is composed of representatives from every process step. This is, in a sense, a team of teams. The functions represented by this group have, as a whole, a definable, measurable target. Within the framework of this team, the chain of supplier-customer relationships is maintained: here problems are dealt with and changes are made.

Step 8: Implementing Valid Scorekeeping
Methods to Eliminate Subjectivity

Scorekeeping is a vital part of Integrated Quality Management. That's why I'm devoting two entire chapters to the subject later in this book.

Don't Forget the Quality Image!

Identifying the customer goal, translating it into the process, and establishing supplier-customer relationships within the process are all actions by which Quality Age firms produce consistently superior products and services.

But throughout this never-ending cycle, the Quality Age firm never loses sight of the fact that quality is also image and perception. As we define the customer goal, set targets within our process, and handle the problems and conflicts that will inevitably arise, we have to assess the impact each decision will have on our quality image. The quality image is not a one-time concern; it is a continuing one.

Benefits of the Transformation

The Quality Age steps that I've outlined have produced a real transformation among firms that were previously in stagnation. But it doesn't happen overnight. You can't learn the customer goal over the weekend, translate it into the process by Wednesday, have your teams up and running by Friday, and drop final inspection the next week.

Such unrealistic expectations practically guarantee failure. And there is a lot more to learn, besides. But with persistence, patience, and thoroughness, any firm—even one enmired, seemingly hopelessly, in stagnation—can realize almost immediate benefits from the steps I've outlined. And the long-term transformation will bring benefits that are truly profound.

- *Reaction to change will be fast and effective.* First of all, by constantly asking questions, you will learn about changes as they happen—not well after the fact. Then the internal communication network will utilize employees' collective knowledge and skill to adapt to those changes in a way that keeps the product or service focused on the customer goal. The system will build on workers' natural desire to excel. It will foster an atmosphere in which workers think about what they're doing, question what's happening, work together toward constant improvement.

- *It will be possible to force change.* As the firm progresses toward leadership in its marketplace, it will be as necessary to *force* change as it is to react to it. Once again, the internal and external communication network established by the steps I've listed will make possible clear-eyed precision plans and actions. The desire to force change will develop quite naturally from the work force's awakened desire to improve and to excel.

- *Quality will be built in, final inspection eliminated.* The process will now consist of well-defined supplier-customer relationships. Each will know what to expect and what to deliver. Motivated by solid feedback and effective score-keeping, each will strive constantly to solve problems, avoid defects, and minimize variation. Final inspection, once a necessary last resort, will become glaringly redundant and will, in time, end.

- *Productivity will improve.* This will happen almost by definition. Reductions in variation equal improved quality, which in turn means that there won't be as much "doing things over." Less variation also leads to increased operating speed, since fewer adjustments are needed.

- *The customer goal will be transcended.* Stagnant firms are always playing "me-too" or "catch-up." As they begin to practice the steps of Integrated Quality Management, they'll be doing less and less of this. In time, they begin to meet the customer goal consistently as it changes; then they acquire the ability to perceive its trends and anticipate it with ever-better products and services. This is the essence of the competitive edge.

In sum, the Quality Age firm is built upon communication. It gets feedback from the outside world on the customer goal and its performance. Then it translates that feedback into meaningful action within a process that is a cohesive communication network in its own right, geared to excellence. The result is customers whose expectations are always met and often exceeded, customers who boast.

Thus far, we've talked about how Quality Age firms establish comunication with customers on the one hand and within the process on the other. We have discussed ways to tear down the walls that induce stagnation. But there's one more entity to talk about—an entity as important as the customers and the process, an entity without which no firm could exist but from which the stagnant firm is separated by a wall as strong as any other. That entity is the supplier network.

To Quality Age firms, suppliers are *partners*, not adversaries. How have they brought such a high level of quality into their supplier relationships?

3

Suppliers:
Where Quality Begins

What can be more exciting than the trapeze act at the circus? No doubt, your heart shoots to your throat as you watch the acrobat swing 30 feet above solid ground . . . release the bar . . . spin and tumble through the air . . . and then, at that critical moment before an inevitable plunge to earth, grab the rescuing hands of the holder who's swung across at precisely the right instant.

Acrobats get all the attention, all the glory. They wear the flashiest costumes, stay in the spotlights, take the bows, bask in applause at the end. Holders, on the other hand, seem almost incidental. But if you ask an acrobat which is the more important, the answer will be "the holder"!

It's easy to see why. The acrobat's skills are certainly impressive. Endless hours of thought and practice go into the design and perfection of the act. But the holder possesses the most critical skill. The acrobat's timing and precision may vary by minute degrees, but the holder's must not. He must be observant beyond belief and blessed with impeccable timing. If the holder errs, even by so little as a nanosecond, down goes the acrobat, *splat*.

The acrobat makes a daily practice of checking in with the holder. He cares about how well fed the holder is, how rested, how confident. He cares more about the holder than about anything else, because his health—if not his life—is in the

48

holder's hands. Without absolute confidence in the holder, the acrobat will never go on.

In an admittedly less vivid way, that same relationship exists in the business world. Your firm is the star of the show. You stand in the spotlight, applying all your skill, effort, and experience. You seek applause in the form of market share, profits, customer loyalty. But in this "act" of sorts, your firm is not, in the final analysis, the most important component.

The most important is the "holder," which is, in this scenario, your supplier force—the firms from which you acquire the products and services needed to produce your own products and services. Now more than ever, your welfare depends on that of your suppliers.

There was a time, during the Invention Age, when this was not so true. Many firms produced their products and services literally from the dust of the earth. For example, Henry Ford was a strong believer in vertical integration. His Rouge River manufacturing complex, at one time the largest such complex in the world, is a monument to that: iron ore in one end, finished autos out the other. Ford bought up the process all the way back to the basic raw materials, iron ore and rubber trees. Ford even bought the railroad by which ore was delivered to his plant. He was determined to control everything.

With rare exceptions, such vertical integration has become a thing of the past. It's just not practical in most cases. As your company becomes larger, its overhead base tends to grow, rendering ancillary products that you make substantially more expensive than those you acquire from outsiders. External sources tend to be leaner, more competitive, more up-to-date, more expert than you can hope to be. Today's firms, especially Quality Age ones, have learned to "stick to the knitting."

You therefore see firms like Ford acquiring some 70 percent of their components from outsiders. Toyota's number is in excess of 80 percent. The percentage for service firms—restaurants, hospitals, insurance operations, and the like—tends to be even higher.

Recognizing this, the Quality Age firm reaches an inescapable conclusion: to produce quality products and services, it must be supplied with quality products and services. This in turn requires an intimate, dynamic relationship with suppliers—the kind of relationship that is common among Quality Age firms and rare among stagnant ones.

Back in the early 1980s, I was an executive for a Fortune 100 firm that manufactured timing chains for automobile engines. Our biggest customers were, as you might expect, the Big Three automakers. One of those automakers was notoriously difficult to deal with, especially when it came to negotiating pricing.

At one point we were supplying timing chains to the automaker at a price of $4.40 each. This had been the price for a long time, and it was no longer adequate. Our studies showed that our material costs had gone up 10 percent. So had labor costs. We had to have a price increase, so after much internal discussion we petitioned the automaker for a 10 percent price increase—44 cents per chain.

After an interminable wait, the automaker called us in for a meeting. The manager in charge sat at a desk, nearly invisible behind a massive computer printout.

"You're in luck," I heard him say.

"How's that?" I responded.

"Our analytic committee has reviewed your price increase request," he said.

"And?"

"It's found that you are indeed eligible for a price increase," the manager announced.

"Well, that's good," I said, relieved.

"You're entitled to an increase of six cents per chain."

"Six?" I asked. "But we put in for 44."

"Six cents," he replied. "That's what the analytic committee has determined that you qualify for. However, what we've decided to give you is . . ."

"Yes?" I asked hopefully.

"Four cents."

What a jam! This was our largest customer. We couldn't live without its business. Time for some real salesmanship, I thought. "Let's talk about this."

"Four cents," the manager said. "That's final."

"I don't know where you get your numbers, but there's . . ."

"The analytic committee put it all together," he told me.

It sounded as if the analytic committee was trying to analyze us right out of business. "Exactly how did they arrive at four cents?" I asked.

He patted the huge computer printout affectionately. "It's all in here. Take it with you if you like. Look it over. Get back to us."

Well, we took the report with us, and we looked at it, and we got back to the automaker. We haggled over the matter for 18 months, I kid you not. With no interim price increase, I might add. In the end we got a higher price: a bit higher than four cents, a lot lower than 44.

The Problem with Price

As a supplier, our relationship with this customer was based on one thing: price. Every other issue was subordinate to it. The same philosophy is followed by today's stagnant firms. The worth of a supplier relationship is directly related to the price charged. Other issues pale into insignificance.

To stagnant firms, there's no such thing as too many suppliers. For any given product or service, purchasers line up a host of potential suppliers: the more the merrier. Multiple suppliers ensure a reliable supply, the thinking goes. Further, multiple suppliers can be played against each other. Such competition supposedly ensures the lowest possible price.

Purchasing people are always on the hunt for victories in the form of price concessions. By playing supplier A against supplier B, they may be able to force a price cut of, say, a penny a pound. This amounts to tremendous savings over a year's time and make heroes of the purchasers. They can extend their victory by using that concession to force similar concessions from other suppliers. The "savings" mount and mount.

But do they? Really? Does that penny-per-pound "savings" go to the bottom line? I don't think so. Here's why.

High Overhead

The more suppliers you use, the more you spend in your purchasing activity. That's just common sense. You need more people who spend more time cutting purchase orders, making phone calls, and haggling. These people need administrative and clerical support, space, equipment, and supplies. Each supplier you deal with adds to your overhead—much more than you probably realize.

Contentious Relationships

Relationships based on price are by definition contentious. The squabbling over nickels and dimes dominates, leaving no time or motivation for the vendor and supplier to care about other concerns. An air of secretiveness pervades the relationship. Your suppliers, knowing you're dealing with their competition, don't dare tell you how they're doing, what their plans are.

In the end, this costs both supplier and customer. Neither side gets the benefit of the other's knowledge and experience. At best, the relationship is arm's-length, defined by dollars and cents.

Forced Compromises in Quality

Often the price-based relationship puts the supplier between a financial rock and a hard place. It can't afford to lose your business, nor can it afford to sell at the price you require. Something has to give, and what always gives first is quality.

To protect profitability, the supplier finds ways to cut corners and make compromises. You may think you're getting the same product or service at a cheaper price, but odds are you're not. "Cheaper," yes; "the same," no. Your purchaser may not be aware of this, but people elsewhere in the organization certainly are.

Minimal Research and Development Support

The supplier who earns only nominal profit on your business has neither the resources nor the incentive to engage in the kinds of research and development that can improve the product or service you are buying. in the end, you pay the penalty for this.

Distance from the Process

When purchasing is based on price, purchasers are separate from the process that actually deals with the acquired products or services. For the most part, they're ignorant of the process itself—how it works and what its needs are. They deal with blueprints, spec sheets, lists of cold, hard facts, and divorce themselves as much as possible from any feedback, wishing to be undistracted from the paramount objective: acquiring things cheaply. This creates the most expensive impact of all.

Increased Processing Cost

When purchasing is done blindly on the basis of price, the result can create havoc within your process. The people who must use the supplied product or service are constantly dealing with the unexpected. This takes two forms:

- The characteristics of the product or service just aren't consistent with the requirements of the process.
- Even worse, the characteristics of the product or service *vary* constantly.

There's our old enemy again: variation! Some variation is natural and avoidable, but much of it isn't. When you buy from many suppliers, or simply buy on the basis of price, you're inviting variation in the door—with disastrous and expensive results.

Let's look at the pizza business for a minute to illustrate how expensive variation in a supplied product can be. Domino's

Pizza founder Tom Monaghan is very strict about how Domino's Pizza looks and tastes. Here, for example, are his requirements for the application of pizza sauce:

> If the sauce is spread too thin, the pizza will taste bland. If it's too thick, the spices will be overpowering. [The sauce must be spread] exactly to within one-half to five-eighths of an inch from the rim, so there's no gap around the edges, and it will look as smooth and level as a jewel in a Swiss watch.[7]

How's that for strict? These requirements require a high degree of skill on the part of the person doing the "saucing." Domino's prizes such skills and holds regular contests among its pizza makers, culminating in an annual Domino's Pizza Olympics.

But all that skill is for naught if the sauce isn't made *correctly* and *consistently*. If it's too thick, there won't be enough in the prescribed portion (one or two spoonsful) to cover the pizza evenly. This means the saucer will have to either use more than the prescribed amount, which costs money and may create an overpoweringly spicy taste that could harm the quality image, or spread it too thinly, creating an unappealing appearance and weak taste that hurts the quality image even more.

"Too thick" or "too thin" are problems, but as long as such deviations are consistent, the saucers can deal with them. What is really damaging is sauce that is inconsistent—that *varies* from batch to batch.

Such variation requires the saucers to adjust what they're doing constantly. These adjustments slow them up, which costs money. Adjusting is never perfect, which also costs money.

The cost of acquiring a supplied product or service is far, far more than just the purchase price; it's the *cost to process that product through your system*. In the end, a purchaser who saves a penny a gallon on sauce that is of capricious consistency—thick here, runny there—ends up costing the firm many thousands of dollars in excessively high processing costs.

Much of this cost is the result of adjustments that have to be made to compensate for this variation. But even more expensive is, as I've said before and will repeat constantly, *damage done to the quality image* when the customer receives pizza that is so thick and pungent it burns the roof of his mouth or so thin and bland it tastes like ketchup on a cracker.

Quality Age firms know that variation is a central cause of quality problems. Integrated quality management therefore makes *reduction of variation* a central goal.

Quality Age firms also recognize that the process doesn't begin at their own front doors. It really begins with the firms that supply the products and services. Quality Age firms don't buy blindly on the basis of price; employ multiple suppliers; and maintain remote, arm's-length relationships with them. They know that such actions invite variation into the process at its earliest, most critical step.

Purchasing in Quality Age firms is, therefore, no longer as simple a matter as picking up the phone and asking "How much will it cost? How fast can I get it?"

Establishing a Quality Age Relationship

The first step that Quality Age firms take toward establishing partnership relationships with suppliers is, quite simply, to reduce the number of suppliers. In particular, they reduce, if not eliminate, multiple suppliers for any particular product or service.

As a key part of its recovery, Ford did exactly that. In 1981, Ford was purchasing from around 8,000 supplier firms. Today, it has cut that number in half without reducing the actual amount of outsourcing. This effort has improved quality by reducing variation in the supplied product. Executives from the firm's Batavia transmission plant tell me that the quality of their product has improved some 400 percent over the past five years and is now rated better than the identical transmission made by Mazda. Part of this improvement is due to decreased variation in the transmission components Ford acquires from outsiders.

Ford's purchasing function has become the envy of the industry. Significantly, Lee Iacocca's regime at Chrysler has made a point of "raiding" Ford's purchasing executives—part of the phenomenon that has led Detroit insiders to refer to Chrysler as the "Gang of Ford."

Another positive effect of reducing the supplier force is that it enables you to establish *close partnership relationships*. These permit you and your suppliers to improve mutually.

This is as important in service businesses as in manufacturing. Tom Monaghan repeatedly credits close supplier relation ships as a key element in the success of Domino's Pizza. He says,

> [An] element in our ability to compete is the support furnished by Domino's suppliers and we work hard to make our association with them mutually beneficial. I'm particularly sensitive to the importance of suppliers because they helped me a great deal over the years.[8]

When you're close to your suppliers, you learn from them and they learn from you. This ongoing effort improves things quickly.

Back in my timing chain days, we were having problems with the steel we were buying for the timing chains we made. We discovered that the steel was actually coming in dirty, with a high incidence of what we called "nonmetallic inclusions," some 130,000 to 140,000 per square inch.

When I complained to our purchasing people, they suggested that we wash the steel. Impractical. Finally, after a lot of hectoring from me, our purchasing people reported the problem to the steel supplier. And almost at once the count of nonmetallic inclusions dropped to about 8,000 per square inch, which was acceptable.

All we had to do was talk to our supplier's people, let them know what we wanted, and the product they sent us improved. Such dialogue is much easier with a small number of suppliers.

But reducing suppliers is not so simple a matter as making a list and lining out every third one. You have to find the right supplier and develop the right sort of relationship—and that takes planning, time, and (here's that word again) consistency.

How to Get the Right Suppliers

The method I've seen used most often is an intelligent mix of the carrot and the stick. The driving philosophy is "If it's good for us, it must be good for our suppliers." In other words, we open ourselves up to them—requiring, in turn, that they open themselves up to us.

Our supplier efforts begin not *after* we've commenced our own improvement program but while we're developing it. The first step is to *get the purchasing function involved*. The communication process we talked about in Chapter 2—identifying the customer goal, communicating it back into the process, and redefining the process into supplier-customer relationships— definitely includes the purchasing function.

In effect, your purchasers are suppliers to some defined number of other functions. They must know what to supply; those being supplied must know what to expect. Feedback between them is essential; therefore, purchasers play a key role in the teams that you develop. They are also intimately involved in scorekeeping.

When purchasers have a clear view of what they are expected to supply, they will quite naturally look at their own sources—the outside suppliers—in a completely new way. Cost of acquisition will remain an issue, but purchasers will be aware of variation, the *cost of processing supplied product through the system*, and be rated on their ability to acquire products and services that consistently meet the needs of their own customers. Then your purchasing department and your firm as a whole will be ready to proceed with steps designed to establish the supplier partnership relationship that is so important.

The next step is to *advise all existing suppliers of your new improvement program*. This can be done in the form of a letter, or, what is even more effective, you can make it the subject of a supplier conference. Whatever you do, be open and clear about your program, the steps you're taking, and the results you expect in terms of fulfilling customer needs, improving quality, and reducing variation.

Advise them that they'll be seeing significant changes in the way you do business, and make it plain that this is a "forever" commitment on your part. (This is a good way to help assure that it stays that way; smokers, for example, find it easier to quit forever once they've told their family and friends.)

An absolutely vital step is to *offer them your assistance with improvement programs of their own.* Offer to recommend sources of assistance, to share results, to confer with them about problems.

Now to the most critical step: *negotiate long-term sole-source contracts with selected suppliers.* Ford Motor Company has taken this step with its supplier force. Its contracts tend to run three years or more—virtually unheard-of in an industry where multiple suppliers and short-term contracts were previously the norm.

The details of such contracts will vary from firm to firm and even, to a degree, from supplier to supplier, but here are the essential elements:

1. *Specifics of the supplied product or service.* Reach agreement with the supplier on more than just how many to ship and how much to charge. Work out a consensus on the characteristics you expect, the consistency of form and function, and the timeliness of delivery.

2. *Commitment to quality improvement program.* The supplier must agree, as a condition of the contract, to implement a full-range quality improvement program. This must be done at its own expense. As part of the arrangement, you will agree to provide advice, counsel, and information on sources of outside assistance.

3. *Reporting requirements.* You will require the supplier to report, in a timely manner, progress in the implementation of its quality improvement program. The supplier should report on such things as numbers of workers trained; regular capability studies; improvements in its own productivity; status of its own suppliers' improvement programs. You will reserve the right to send audit teams to the suppliers' facilities to examine the progress first-hand (an activity that is pursued aggressively by Ford and others).

4. *Pricing concessions.* Built into the contract will be a structure of steady price declines. This is predicated on the expectation that the suppliers' improvement program, if properly and vigorously implemented, will result in significant cost savings over the life of the contract. These cost savings are not confined to the supplied product itself; they will also occur through reduction in the supplier's administrative overhead. You expect to share in these savings through the gradual price declines.

5. *Most-favored-nation status.* The supplier is not prohibited from doing business with your competitors, but it must agree not to sell to your competitors at a price lower than the price at which it sells to you.

6. *Indemnification.* The sole-source agreement must protect you from the risk that the supplier may be unable to provide its product due to strikes, disasters, or other occurrences. The supplier must give formal assurance that the product will be furnished to you on the agreed-upon basis, whatever may occur.

As you might expect, many suppliers hesitate to enter into such sole-source relationships. Some reject the notion out of hand. Some view it as an unwarranted intrusion. Some see it as a you-win, they-lose proposition. To that you can reply only by citing indisputable facts:

1. *The supplier will get all your business, which means higher volume.* Here you can and should give a forecast, backed up with your total purchase history of the product or service under discussion. The supplier's sales force will see the benefit of that immediately. To the supplier, you will represent a secure source of sales.

2. *The supplier earns higher profits from economies of scale.* In many cases, higher volume means higher profit per unit and improved overall profitability for the supplier.

3. *You'll share research and development activities.* Because you'll be working much more closely together, the supplier will benefit from your input. Like you, the supplier needs to learn the customer goal in order to succeed.

Under this program, you'll be sharing your understanding on an ongoing basis. This input will help your supplier develop other products and services.

4. *You'll provide assistance in quality and productivity improvement.* Each supplier is a firm like yours and mine: concerned about improving quality and productivity, concerned about prospects for survival and growth in the Quality Age. By working closely with you, your supplier will gain priceless expertise in the improvement process, expertise with which it can transform its own organization. By working with you, each supplier will learn how to increase its overall competitive strength in the Quality Age.

5. *The supplier will benefit from dramatic reductions in costs.* Improved quality can increase operating speed, which translates into higher productivity and lower costs. Reduced variation lowers costs also, particularly in scrap and rework. But the savings don't end there; the supplier will enjoy reduced advertising and marketing expenses, by virtue of its reliance on your business for the contract period. And, as Integrated Quality Management spreads to encompass all aspects of the operation, it will experience lower administrative and overhead costs.

6. *The national trend is toward sole-sourcing.* Ford is an example I've cited before, but it's not alone. Sole-sourcing has taken hold in the entire auto-industry, and has spread to many non-automotive firms such as Campbell's, Peterbilt, Boeing, and Douglas.

7. *The global trend is toward sole-sourcing.* Japanese companies have interrelated on this basis for many years. The result is clear. Japan has become an economic juggernaut—a national economic network that has stormed ashore in America and elsewhere. Each Quality Age firm knows that it is, at once, a supplier and a customer. No firm is an island; none operates in a vacuum. To survive and grow, all of us must work more closely together.

8. *Ultimately, the relationship will strengthen the supplier.* True, Ford cut its supplier base in half, but those that remain

are, by far, stronger, more vigorous and more successful as a result.

Even when you have outlined these benefits to your supplier force, some of them will drop out of the running. That should be no cause of concern to you. In this way, your sole-sourcing proposition gives you a glimpse into the future. It shows you who is likely to survive and who is likely to fail.

A word of caution: Some suppliers will seem agreeable to the conditions of the arrangement, and then, after the contract begins, they won't follow through 100 percent. They'll pay a great deal of lip service; then they'll send late reports, flimsy analyses, downright bogus information on their program—a royal snow job, in other words.

That's why it's essential to follow through as Ford has done. Keep a wary eye on the quality of the supplied product and its adherence to the target values as well as the degree of variation around those target values. Vigorously analyze the information you get from suppliers on the progress of their improvement programs. Send audit teams periodically to review the suppliers' programs on the spot. This is the only way you can be sure that the suppliers are living up to their end of the deal.

By being all at once supportive, demanding, and watchful of your suppliers, you'll see them fall into line eventually. Even the suppliers who start out trying to snow you will change their ways. They'll find that it's easier to get serious about an effective Quality Age improvement program than it is to maintain a convincing pretense.

And once they've embarked as seriously upon improvement as you have and experienced some of the early successes they'll wonder why they ever tried to snow you in the first place.

What's in It for You

We've talked in detail about how sole-sourcing benefits Quality Age suppliers. Now let's look at the ways sole-sourcing benefits you, the Quality Age firm.

1. *Security.* You will have a reliable, dependable source for the supplied product or service. Your purchasing people will be relieved of the pressure to shop the market, sometimes on a last-minute, panic basis (which leads to mistakes).

2. *Reduced variation.* Today, in an effort to prevent a defective supplied product from getting into your system, you may be spending a lot of money on inspection. Under the new relationship, you'll be able to dispense with that eventually. By implementing its own improvement program, your supplier will reduce its variation and improve its quality. If everyone is doing his or her job, the product you receive should be absolutely consistent with your expectations. It won't be perfect. But it will meet your variation expectations around the target value that you and the supplier have mutually established.

   This lowers cost to you at the front end by eliminating preinspection. It also improves quality within your own process because you will no longer have to compensate for supplier variation by making expensive adjustments. This in turn reduces processing time, increasing operating speed and improving productivity.

3. *Guaranteed pricing and price adjustments.* When the supplier guarantees pricing over an extended period of time, your financial planning will become much easier. Further, you can look forward to lower costs as the supplier's own costs decrease through better quality and efficiency. You will have broken the historic and seemingly endless price increase spiral.

4. *Greater supplier dependence.* Just as you'll depend more on the supplier, the supplier will depend more upon you. You will be a much more important player among the supplier's cadre of customers. The supplier will inevitably be more responsive to your needs, more receptive to your suggestions and ideas. The relationship will become constantly smoother, and smooth relationships are the secret ingredient of successful businesses.

5. *Expanded research and development abilities.* By working with the supplier on the design side, you'll find your own product development cycle becoming smoother and more successful. You won't be creating products and services in as much of a vacuum as you do now; you'll have a much better feel for the supplier's capabilities, be able to take advantage of its expertise, reduce costly rework and startover, and shorten the cycle time between concept and introduction.

   In the early days of Domino's Pizza, the firm had trouble with the pizza boxes it was acquiring. No one's product satisfied Domino's exacting requirements, and none of its existing suppliers seemed anxious to go the extra mile. Domino's founder Tom Monaghan cites the extended, painstaking efforts of a young, hungry box supplier as the reason for Domino's success in coming up with a box that was state-of-the-art in the business.

6. *The ability to implement a just-in-time system.* When your supplier's quality is unpredictable, you inevitably fall into the habit of over-ordering to make sure that you end up with as much good product as you'll need. Under this program, your supplier's product will improve constantly. You'll be able to order smaller quantities more frequently. This will reduce your level of investment in raw goods, floor space, and other overhead items. You'll be able to implement a just-in-time ordering system, which is not at all feasible unless the supplier's quality and efficiency is consistent and predictable.

7. *Better communication.* Today, the atmosphere of customer-supplier relationships tends to be tense and guarded, if not adversarial and confrontational. Under a sole-sourcing arrangement, the general atmosphere will improve greatly. You will both be working toward a common goal—your mutual betterment. Your mutual improvement program will give you a common language. You'll understand each other's needs. You'll become a team.

If you're thinking about implementing Integrated Quality Management in your firm and are wondering at what point you should go to work on establishing the supplier-partner relationships about which I've talked, the answer is *now*. It should be one of the first steps.

As you'll see in the coming chapters, your efforts at internal improvement will focus on reducing variation from stage to stage in your process. You'll be training your workers about variation. For most of them, this will be a brand-new concept. You'll be training them about its causes and solutions. You'll be forming teams and groups. You'll be motivating them to reduce variation through improved scorekeeping and incentive systems.

How can you expect workers to get serious about reducing variation and improving quality within the process if they're forced to work with products that are rife with variation and defects? Ultimately, you can't reduce variation within your process if the products and services coming in at the front end are afflicted with variation. That's why overhauling your supplier relationships is essential.

The sooner you start, the sooner you'll begin to reap the benefits. And there's another reason to get going quickly: You'll get a big edge on your competitors. You don't want them establishing partnership relationships with suppliers before you've done so.

I don't for a moment claim that any of this is easy. It can be tough and even painful. Many of your supplier relationships are, most likely, of long standing. You may feel it's not your place to "dictate" anything to them. But don't lose sight of the central issue here: survival.

To survive, you must be a Quality Age company. That is fact. Being a Quality Age company is as much a matter of vision as it is of execution. And you can't be a Quality Age company if your suppliers don't share that vision.

What would you rather do? Survive and excel with those who share your vision? Or decline and fall with those who don't?

That's your choice. It's that simple.

PART II

QUALITY PEOPLE

For many years, people have argued that the key to improving productivity—yes, and quality too—is automation. Today, computers have taken over labor-intensive tasks in virtually every arena of business. Computers have even begun to take responsibility for some forms of decision making. One example is the stock market, where so-called "program trading" has become common. The Dow takes a 30-point hit, and analysts soberly tell us that the computers did it.

In other arenas, especially manufacturing, robots have taken jobs formerly held by people—principally dangerous or excessively repetitive jobs. Robotics in general is thought to be the coming thing; robots don't call in sick, go on strike, or come to work hung over.

Fair enough. But there seems to be a technological limit to automation. We haven't reached the point yet where unaided computers can manage the robots that do the work. Behind the computers and the robots are people: people who design them, people who tell them what to do, people who watch them. People—managers and workers—are still, in the end, responsible for what happens. People are the heart of the company. The company, its products, and its services are only as good as its people are.

To this point we've examined the role of quality inside and outside stagnant and Quality Age firms. We've shown how Quality Age firms develop a detailed definition of quality in terms of their customers, and we've discussed how to translate that information into the process itself.

All of that is valuable and essential, but it's also meaningless unless we address the all-important human element. Let's look at some ways Quality Age firms inspire a completely new attitude among managers and workers, an attitude that sparks a constant and never-ending drive for improvement.

4

Quality Management

In 1967, I took a summer job as a fire shoveler in a steel mill. I'll never forget reporting to work the first day. I was grateful to have the job—I was in college and needed the money desperately—but the position was light-years off my career path and I felt nervous. That feeling only grew as the situation unfolded.

First, the head of personnel sat me down and showed me a very graphic, grisly movie about a car accident. It depicted the utter obliteration of four people, no holds barred: guts hanging out, arms out of sockets, a smashed brain. When it was over, the head of personnel told me, "We showed you this movie because, here at the mill, *we believe in safety*, and we want you to believe in it too."

Oh, I believed in it all right, with all my heart. So I gladly took each piece of equipment the head of personnel gave me: helmet, goggles, steel-toed shoes. He warned me to wear them at all times. I told him I believed in safety.

I was taken into the mill, and the first thing I saw was the biggest sign I'd ever seen in my life. It must have been 45 feet high by 70 feet wide, and it said, in big bold letters, **WE BELIEVE IN SAFETY**.

The foreman met me and walked me through the mill. The air was hot and filthy, visibility only 75 or 100 feet. It was clear enough for me to see a crane carrying a 20,000-pound steel ingot. It glowed red-hot, dropping fiery little chunks that exploded on the floor around me. As if that wasn't disturbing enough, the crane had such a tenuous hold on the ingot that, even to my inexperienced eyes, it looked as if the ingot could break loose any moment and come crashing to the floor.

I asked the foreman about that. He shrugged. "Well, Ralph's really tired, he's on his third shift, he might drop one or two."

I thought, Is *this* why they insist that I wear a helmet? "My God," I gasped. "What do I do when they drop?"

"That's the least of your worries!"

Well, at least I didn't have to work in that department. I was assigned to the open hearth, where molten steel heated to 2,200 degrees fell out of the pits onto the floor. My job was to shovel it.

We entered that department. Here again was another sign, just as big as the first one. It said:

> This Department #1 in Safety!
> 52 HOURS 30 MINUTES
> Since Last Fatality

The foreman said, "Perry, aren't you glad you're gonna work in the safest department?"

I swallowed hard. "Fifty-two hours, huh?"

"Yep, we're going for the record this year."

"Hope we make it."

"You got to be careful in here, Perry. Remember: we believe in safety."

I noticed a tractor sitting some distance away. Sitting in the driver's seat, protected not only by his helmet but also by a steel canopy over the cab, was the driver, sound asleep.

I pointed him out to the foreman. He said, "Yeah, good old Joe. He's got the life, all right." He looked at me. "You like the looks of that job, huh?"

I sure did. It looked not only easy but safe. And by then, having seen what I'd seen, I really, *really* believed in safety.

"Well, Perry, you play your cards right, someday that job'll be yours. Meanwhile, you gotta put in your time."

I did that, all right. I worked alongside other college kids for better than four weeks, shoveling molten steel in the filthy, dirty 120-degree mill. It was constant work, the hardest, most grueling work I've ever done.

Meanwhile Joe, the tractor driver, only worked maybe 10 minutes out of each hour. And even so his activities barely qualified as work. He'd simply start the tractor, move some steel around, shut the tractor off again, and sleep the other 50 minutes. It was the life—for a while, anyway.

One day one of the pits opened up and all the 2,200-degree molten steel came down and engulfed the tractor, melting it beyond recognition and burning Joe alive.

I was only 60 feet away from him at the time. I ran to the foreman, panicky and frantic. "My God, Joe just got burned alive! The pit opened up and everything fell."

"Dawggone," the foreman said. "We were doing so well. Now Joe's gone and ruined our safety record. Well, he never did have any brains." He looked at me. "What does this mean to you, Perry?"

"Means I'm getting the hell out of here!"

"Oh, no, no, no! Listen to me. Out of every bad thing, there's always some good. And there's some good in this for you. The first day you were here, remember you looked at Joe and I told you something that day. Remember?"

"No."

"I told you if you played your cards right, one day his job would be yours. Well, today's the day!"

"Oh, my God. "

"That job can be yours. All you have to do is say so."

"Oh . . . "

"Pays six cents an hour more, too!"

Needless to say, I didn't volunteer.

Later that year the government threatened to shut the mill down. Why? Because, despite the movie, slogans, signs, helmets, goggles, and steel-toed shoes, the government decided that the mill had a safety problem.

Top Management—Where the Buck Stops

That mill preached safety, yet practiced something quite different. Likewise, most of today's stagnant firms preach "all the right things"—quality, productivity, worker involvement, fulfillment of customer expectations—yet do things that are directly contrary.

Who's responsible? Management. Especially top management. Management not only runs the firm; management *is* the firm. Management establishes goals and sets examples. Most critical, management controls the money. Management holds the livelihoods of all the workers in its hands.

Part of the price of admission to the Quality Age is accepting the fact that stagnant firms became stagnant due to management—not unions, the government, import policies, or anything else. Poor management can only drive a firm into stagnation. It takes the unswerving commitment of an enlightened management to pull a firm out of stagnation and maintain the dynamism of the Quality Age firm.

That's one of the toughest selling jobs I've ever had to perform. Too often, troubled firms get fired up about the philosophies and techniques of Integrated Quality Management—then cut the effort off at the knees by announcing that they're going to improve "from the bottom up." Lasting change, true lasting improvement starts with top management and works its way down, not the other way around.

There are two major reasons that top management must commit itself first: top management's effect on middle management and its control of the system.

Middle Management Follows
Top Management's Lead

I've heard many clients blame middle management for the failure of their improvement programs. Middle management can certainly kill the improvement program, but only if top management is not doing its job.

Middle managers tend to resist quality and productivity improvement efforts because they feel threatened. They see that the new programs—teams, feedback, scorekeeping, and the rest—drive decision making downward. Middle managers feel that the program costs them authority and status.

But their resistance is surprisingly easy to change. Middle management is, in fact, the most pliable and least intransigent worker group! After all, to whom do middle managers report? Top managers. Whose expectations do middle managers have to live up to? Top managers'. What jobs do middle managers aspire to? You guessed it. Middle managers want to get promoted. To do that, they have to please top managers. Most middle managers are very adept at this.

Here's how the top managers of Quality Age firms bring middle managers into line and enlist their solid support for the improvement program:

- They set a positive, consistent example. If top managers pay lip service to the program, you can rest assured middle managers will too.

- They're as responsive to middle managers' ideas and suggestions as middle managers are expected to be to the ideas and suggestions of workers reporting to them.

- They change the goal structure. Top managers should set objectives for middle managers that directly reflect the firm's new goals: quality, productivity, reduction of variation, customer satisfaction. Each middle manager should perceive a direct relationship between personal goals and the firm's goals.

- They evaluate middle managers' performance against these goals in specific, measurable terms. This performance should be the criterion for salary increases and promotions. At Ford, Improvement of Quality is frequently found as an item in performance appraisals—and sometimes it represents as much as 50% of the total appraisal.

- They compensate for the perceived reduction in middle management authority by consistently recognizing middle managers ose areas achieve or exceed their goals.

When top management does all these things, middle management falls into line with surprising speed. But only top management can make it happen. In the following section, you'll see why.

Top Management Controls the System

I've heard many clients blame the workers for poor quality and for the failure of improvement programs. This is nothing but an alibi. Poor quality is the fault not of line and hourly workers but of *the system in which they work.*

Top management—not the workers—governs the system. It's up to management to respond to system problems and effect remedies. Workers can't do that. All they can do is report the problems, which, I've found, workers are all to eager to do—if management will only listen. Here are some examples:

- A fastener plant in Kentucky hired me to help improve its quality and productivity. One particular problem involved an indenting operation. Workers seemd unable to produce indentations at the required 90 to 110 inch-pounds of breakaway torque. I had them produce five consecutive parts, and upon measurement we found that the five ranged from 40 to 140 inch-pounds of torque despite the workers' best efforts. Clearly, the machine was in serious need of an overhaul. It was a system problem, but management had been convinced that it was a worker problem.

- A Michigan firm asked me to help with its quality problems. The circuit boards it manufactured had devastating quality problems. My study determined that the problem was not the assembly operation at all but defective transistors acquired on the outside. Once again, it was a system problem, not a worker problem.

The communications network built into an Integrated Quality Management program brings all types of system problems to top management's attention. If top managers don't deal with these problems openly and effectively, they will, I guarantee, kill the program before it gets a good start.

One example of a top executive who takes quality responsibility seriously is Sam Johnson, chairman of Johnson Wax. In the true Quality Age tradition, Johnson Wax's middle managers take quality seriously. Why? Because they know that Sam does. They know that the workers do. They know that workers have been known to call Sam Johnson personally—even at his home, at night—if any quality problem goes unsolved. In fact, every year Sam Johnson gets several such calls from people on his production floor.

There's no substitute for top management commitment such as this. I know that from personal experience. On many occasions, I've been asked to help clients improve quality by training line workers only—not line foremen, supervisors, or middle managers, let alone top management. Those "bottom-up" programs always die.

Now I don't even accept assignments from firms whose top management isn't committed to the program from the beginning. It just isn't worth it.

Getting Top Management Commitment

Some executives, like Sam Johnson, whose "name is on the building," become committed to improvement quite early. In other cases, I've found that top management is only cautiously enthusiastic about Integrated Quality Management, but not fully committed. How can you enlist the wholehearted commitment of top management that is essential for success?

Step 1: Hold a Management Indoctrination Session

This initial step is a kind of "reality adjustment" that absolutely must be conducted by an outsider, a consultant with broad experience in firms of all kinds and a sterling professional reputation.

Why an outsider? First, the right person will have unquestioned credibility. Second, and most important, the person has no employment ties with the firm. With nothing to lose, he or she can be brutally frank and "tell it like it is." An outsider will be unafraid to butt heads, explode pet ideas, debunk the cherished myths that are rife within stagnant firms.

W. Edwards Deming, the near-legendary quality improvement consultant, is notorious for leaving top management groups pale and shaken up after telling them in straight langugage what's *really* going on in their ailing firms. One of his most effective efforts was with the Ford Motor management group in 1980, and the results are plain for all to see.

I myself have performed that valuable service many times. In the indoctrination session, I discuss most of the topics taken up in this book: the Quality Age, the customer goal, improvement as a survival issue, reorienting supplier relations, the need for effective scorekeeping, and the irreplaceable role of top management commitment.

I speak bluntly about their firm's struggle, and what's in store for them if they don't improve. And, on the brighter side, I talk about success stories—how others have improved and what results they might expect for themselves—as outlined in the following section.

Step 2: Get Educated on Success Stories

The only top managers who are totally unaware of corporate success stories in the past 20 years are those who've been in hibernation. But mere awareness is not enough. I've found that top managers take others' experiences to heart. When they're educated on the successes of other firms, they become enthusiastic about their own programs. So I always bring up specific examples.

Take Japan, for example. It went from the devastation of 1945 to today's third-largest economic power—with nothing like America's abundant natural resources, only half our population, and land area the size of the state of Montana!

I also use some specific examples from my own experience. For example, at one of my seminars in Ford's Batavia transmission plant, executives told me that this facility improved its productivity by 400 percent and its quality, in terms of variation reduction, by an even larger margin. Now Ford feels that their transmission is even better than the identical model made by Mazda.

Other firms, large and small, also qualify: Federal-Mogul; Romeo Rim; Modern Hardchrome, where an improvement program literally saved the firm; and the subsistence area of the U.S. Navy Physical Distribution Center, where a carefully implemented Integrated Quality Management program improved productivity by some 132 percent and quality went from 97% to 99.3% in one year.

Success stories abound, and learning about them is vital to obtain top management commitment.

Step 3: Get a Feel for the Tangible Improvements They Can Expect

Studies are available that give a clear, if general, view of the kinds of improvements that stagnant firms can expect to see with the techniques of Integrated Quality Management. From my own experience, I tell top managements they can expect

- Productivity to increase at least 10 percent in the first 12 months, when all the pieces are in place.
- Scrap and rework to be reduced by 20 percent, as a very conservative estimate, the first year. The results here have been even better, depending on circumstances such as dependence on outside suppliers.
- Overall variation to be reduced by 25 percent within the first year.
- New product/service cycle time to be cut in half within two years.
- The firm's Quality Image to improve steadily.

Step 4: Have Top Management Undergo Training in IQM Methods

This is the ultimate in example setting—the best way for top managers to "put your money where your mouth is." Nothing reduces worker suspicion and resentment more than seeing the big bosses undergo the same training that they're requiring of the workers. Moreover, the training gives top management an irreplaceable feel for how the system works. It helps them understand the reports and the results they'll be getting.

Once again, examples show the way: at Ford Motor Company, chairman Donald Petersen has taken training in Statistical Process Control and mandates it for the rest of Ford's management. The same is true at other firms I've worked with: Litton, Westinghouse, Crown Cork & Seal, and Johnson Wax. Even the U. S. Navy has followed this example. The chief of the Navy's worldwide physical distribution operation, Admiral Walker, attended a briefing on SPC and required SPC training of the officers who reported to him.

Quality Age Management Style

The four steps I've outlined will, in most cases, put top management squarely behind the total improvement program. But, as with everything else, commitment can fade unless it is constantly reinforced by the practice of what I call a *Quality Age management style*.

The activities listed in this section are commonly practiced by the top management of Quality Age firms. By conducting them consistently throughout the firm, management can achieve two important objectives.

The first is to *erase worker skepticism*. Often, stagnant firms have taken stabs at improvement programs before, sometimes more than once. After the period of "sound and fury" that I've mentioned before, the programs fade away.

Just telling workers that "we're turning over a new leaf" isn't enough. They've seen that leaf turned so many times, it's become tattered and threadbare. Their skepticism won't change overnight, and enthusiasm can't be dictated by top management. It can be generated only by distinct changes in management practice and style.

The second objective is to *renew and reinforce management commitment*. Managment, as a group, sets examples for itself as well as for the work force. Management can't change the firm, revitalize and transform it, without changing the way it does things too.

Here is how you can develop a Quality Age management style.

Be Consistent in All Things

My youthful experience in the steel mill is the most egregious example of inconsistency that I've ever seen. "We believe in safety"—with workers droping like flies!

But in subsequent years I've seen uncountable other examples of management inconsistency, such as:

- One of my early corporate jobs was with a huge firm that made radiators. Though we had strict quality policies, the inspection procedures we employed were often a worthless joke. Ultimately, whether a product got shipped or not depended on the urgency of the order, not on the quality of what we made. We counted the "leakers" but shipped them anyway if the customer was screaming for delivery loudly enough.

- I once implemented a quality training program for a fastener maker that involved only the line workers (which, as you know, bodes ill for the program's success). When I made a follow-up visit some time later to assess the firm's progress, the line workers told me that nothing had changed. "We're still shipping junk," one told me. "It's just as bad as before. We'll ship an order when half the product is out of spec, yet hold up another one because three errors were found. Doesn't make sense."

Management, and only management, has the power to eliminate such inconsistencies. And management also has the duty.

Accept the Facts; Don't Kill the Messenger

One of the most complicated assignments I ever undertook was to implement Integrated Quality Management for a major West Coast warehouse/distribution operation.

I began by performing a detailed evaluation of the existing operations. I'll get to some of the specifics later, but, for now, suffice it to say that things were an unbelievable mess, absolutely unbelievable.

My next step was to put together a report summarizing what I'd found along with an IQM plan. I had to present all this information to the executive who was directly responsible for the operation.

As I was developing my report, I shared some of its details with a few of the executive's subordinates. They were shocked, but not that I'd found so many problems—they already knew all the gory details. They were shocked and upset that I intended to share all this with the boss.

"He'll have a stroke!" they told me. "Don't tell him that. He'll have an absolute heart attack."

Of course, in my presentation I was blunt and thorough about my findings. The executive didn't have a heart attack or a stroke or anything else. He just sat there and listened. Afterward, he told me he wasn't really surprised; he'd suspected that the problems were much more extensive than he'd been told.

As I've said, top management sets the commmunication tone for the firm. One thing that separates Quality Age managers from the managers of stagnant firms is their handling of bad news.

In some cases, top management is so passive that a "camouflage" syndrome develops down the line. Bad news gets sanitized, step-by-step, as it comes up the ladder. By the time it reaches the top, it is vague, benign, and meaningless. In these situations, top managers have no real idea of what is happening. They're living in a dream world. They think everything is hunky-dory. The cycle becomes self-fulfilling; now underlings are afraid to break the cycle, rationalizing that "we don't want him to have a heart attack."

Well, I've found that top managers are pretty tough. Otherwise, they don't reach the top. Bad news may upset them, but it usually doesn't surprise them. And if it does, too bad. They can't deal with reality unless they know what it is. And they'll never find out what it is as long as they're ringleaders in a conspiracy of silence.

They'll also never find out what's going on if they're in the habit of "killing the messenger." The conspiracy of silence—"hear no evil, see no evil, speak no evil"—is bad enough. What's worse is when top managers punish the bearers of bad news. They only have to do it once. After that, they never hear it again. But all they're doing is putting off the day of reckoning, postponing problems till it's too late to do anything about them.

When top management begins to accept the facts and deal with reality, a funny thing happens. Workers who've been reporting flagrantly bogus numbers begin to tell the truth. They begin reporting the real levels of quality and productivity even when they're abysmal.

Managers are always astounded when workers actually start *telling on themselves*. They've never seen such a thing happen before. But they accept the facts, swallow hard, and begin to ask the workers what needs to be done to improve. In time, the results are incredible.

Set Realistic and Simple Goals

Say you need to travel from New York to Chicago. Do you book flights from New York to Dallas to Salt Lake City to Atlanta to Chicago? I know that your *luggage* sometimes takes that route, but *you* don't. You book direct.

Such simplicity and directness only makes sense. But that's exactly what's lacking in the plans and goals set by the management of stagnant firms. There's a strong tendency to over-complicate the goal structure. The more complicated it is, the less resemblance it bears to reality. The less real it is, the less likely it is to be understood. The less understood it is, the less likely it is to be achieved. Quality Age firms keep goals simple, and they make sure the goals are real.

As important as sales, profits, and market share are, they are subordinate to customer satisfaction. I can't overstate the importance of determining the customer goal and translating it into tangible goals within the firm. Unless your firm meets those goals, there's no hope of meeting sales, profit, and market share objectives.

Moreover, in the Quality Age, management must drive the message home with the work force—not just once, but constantly and consistently. At Domino's Pizza, Tom Monaghan did exactly that. Having determined that his customers expected top quality pizza and 30-minute delivery, he never let his workers forget it:

I kept harping on these things at every meeting we had. My employees might moan and groan at hearing me repeat them, but I didn't let that bother me. It isn't enough to know what you want: You have to make sure that the people who can get it for you know you want it.[9]

The natural tendency is to complicate. Only management can simplify. In the general course of things, efforts tend to become diffuse. Only management can focus efforts. People are easily sidetracked into irrelevancies. Only management can keep the firm on the direct path. In business, as in sports, the team with the least amount of flash is generally the one that wins.

Maintain High, Yet Realistic Expectations

Suppose you're a 95 golfer, and, as your golfing coach, I want you to shoot 70. I can give you a lengthy pep talk: encouragement, exhortations, promises of reward, even threats of punishment. I can build you up, get you all excited, send you out on the golf course—and what do you shoot? Probably somewhere around 95.

High expectations are an important part of Quality Age management. We always want to look for improvement, expect improvement, expect people to excel and do their best. At the same time, management's expectations have to be realistic. Unrealistic expectations breed barriers and false reporting. They create *bad* communication, which is just the opposite of what we want. We can set high, yet realistic expectations through valid scorekeeping. We'll talk about that later.

Tailor Jobs to Individuals, Not Individuals to Jobs

Let's say we're managing a baseball team, and we have a problem with our third baseman. He's a great hitter and has a great arm, but his legs aren't all that good anymore. He's not as quick as he once was. Some hits are getting through because he isn't covering as much ground at the hot corner as we think he ought to.

As management, what do we do? Do we call him in, lecture him about his defensive problems, order grueling exercise programs to build him up? Do we criticize him and humiliate him, maybe even threaten to fire him when he blows a play?

Of course not. We keep him in the lineup because his throwing arm is deadly when he gets to the ball and his batting breaks games wide open for us. We compensate for his bad legs by getting our shortstop, left fielder, and second baseman to cover more ground. We look at the bigger picture, and we adjust.

Quality Age firms do likewise. Just as entrepreneurships stay loose, flexible, and constantly adjusting, so do Quality Age giants. When we create and enforce rigid job descriptions and expect living, breathing human beings to conform magically to the dictates of a list on a piece of paper, we're hampering the efforts of the individuals and the team both.

Quality Age management takes the time, and does the work, to learn the strengths and weaknesses of its team members—and tailors its plays to maximize their strengths.

Seek Out and Publicize Success Stories

As a kid, I attended Catholic schools, and I'll never forget how the nuns handled test results. They always ranked students by the grades they scored. The top 10 scorers had to stand as their names were announced. So did the 10 *worst* scorers.

What's more, seating order was determined by grade standing. The best students got seats in the front. They were, therefore, known to one and all as the smartest. The worst students got seats in the back. They were, therefore, known to one and all as the dumbest.

I guess the nuns regarded this system as a positive, motivating one. Somehow, I don't think it was—at least not for the students who needed motivation the most.

I see a lot of firms that covertly, and even overtly, humiliate workers who make mistakes, underperform, or fail. I also see a lot of firms investing a lot of time and resources in designing and executing incentive programs to stimulate and reward top performance. Incentive programs can be an effective stimulus. But what's often neglected is another way to stimulate and reward top performance—one that's simple, fun, and virtually free.

Seek out and publicize success stories, no matter how small. Quality Age firms do it all the time. When asked, workers will insist that bonuses, days off, and other rewards are real and preferable to recognition, but the fact is that positive recognition is as stimulating and rewarding as anything else. It appeals to personal pride and competitiveness.

I like to see management become far less stingy with praise and recognition as the Integrated Quality Management program gets under way. I encourage management to make the effort to uncover success stories, even minor ones, and publicize them.

It's important also that the recognition go to the person most directly responsible for the success. Otherwise, you're just shooting yourself in the foot.

I remember one of the wrap-up meetings after I finished implementing IQM at the West Coast warehouse/distribution facility mentioned earlier. The executive giving the report gave credit for the results to the president a total of 74 times. He mentioned the workers only once, and that was when he said that the program would have worked much better "if the workers hadn't been so resistant. " I wanted to kick him.

Foster a Team Spirit

These days there's an awful lot of play being given to the notion of reducing barriers between management and the work force by eliminating executive parking spaces, lunchrooms, and the like. This follows the example of the Japanese and is therefore automatically thought of as a good thing.

I believe that, for all the merits and positive results of the Japanese way of doing things, it can't be abruptly translated to U.S. businesses. That's because of the significant cultural differences between us and the Japanese. In Japan, executives almost always rise from the ranks, having worked for just one firm their entire careers and having held positions in virtually every function of the firm. That's not how it works here, and it would take several generations to change over. The career paths of managers and the workers who report to them are very different.

Don't get the idea that I advocate elitism and the ivory tower approach. I don't. What I'm saying is that cosmetic acts like eliminating executive parking spaces and dining rooms are just that—cosmetic. *Workers* regard them as a joke.

Quality Age managers take steps to erase barriers between management and hourly personnel, increase communication between them, and foster a team spirit, but their steps are more than just cosmetic. In the Quality Age firm, managers don't hide in their offices. They get down in the trenches and meet with hourly workers regularly.

While structured settings are okay, it's just as effective, if not more so, to get out there and talk to people. Learn their names. Get to know them. Let them get to know you. Ask questions. Be curious. Learn from them. And take action on what you learn. Treat them with courtesy, dignity, and respect—the way you like to be treated.

Once again, it's important to do this consistently. A two-minute visit twice a year won't cut it. It needs to be a regular part of the routine—something the hourly personnel come to expect.

By making a habit of this, managers can tap into one of the firm's most valuable resources: ideas. Many ideas won't be workable, but there's nothing wrong with that. As Thomas Edison said, "The way to have a good idea is to have lots of ideas."

That's what management is really all about: the collection and implementation of ideas. To keep the ideas coming, management should also take care to give hourly workers *ownership* of their ideas. This is the "spotlight" technique again, in a slightly different form.

I think managers should work at a 180-degree turnabout from current practice. Let's get away from telling hourly personnel what to do all the time and strive to create an atmosphere where they make many of those decisions for themselves, based on their own ideas. They'll work much harder and more effectively for an idea that they helped to create.

And getting out there to talk with the hourly personnel also gives managers the opportunity to check up and see what's really going on. Nothing replaces this: not report-reading, not even phone calls. You have to get out there. As Tom Monaghan points out:

> You don't get what you *expect* unless you *inspect*. When you ask questions on the telephone, you get the answers you prefer to hear. If you visit the store in person, though, you get thousands of impressions, a lot of them pointing to things that need improvement. When a store is running smoothly, visiting it seems like a waste of time. But just stop visiting that store for a few months, and it will deteriorate dramatically. I learned that lesson the hard way, through experience.[10]

Use Real Numbers from Valid Scorekeeping Systems

Here it is again: scorekeeping! Effective management demands it. In today's stagnant firms, management often relies on numbers that aren't real. For example, let me describe some facets of the scorekeeping system I found at that West Coast warehouse/distribution operation I talked about before.

This facility was almost unimaginably huge. It handled many thousands of different items, from toothpicks to engines, in quantities from one each to many thousands each. In short order, I got a handle on why management was having trouble improving quality and productivity. The scorekeeping systems were, shall we say, somewhat deficient.

Hourly personnel were required to report their daily production. However, because the measurement and scorekeeping system was so nebulous, workers in fact reported what they were told to report. In many cases, the numbers they reported were totally fictitious. One worker told me bluntly, "We're told what numbers to make up."

One standard unit of measurement was something called the "line items per man hour." A *line item* is a single entry on a picking slip. A *man hour* is self-explanatory. The number of line items processed was divided by the number of man hours expended. The problem with this unit of measurement was it was internally inconsistent. It was not a fair representation of the amount of work actually expended.

One line item involved loading 140 pallets (six or seven truckloads) of material. This took several workers a whole day to process. Another line item consisted of a single box. One worker could process 35 to 40 of these line items in an hour.

Another unit of measurement was something called a "measurement ton." Once again, no one seemed to know for sure what it was. One supervisor ventured the notion that a measurement ton was anything that could be put on a skid. A box of toothpicks was therefore a measurement ton. So were 50 crates of apples.

I know this all sounds like something out of a Kafka novel, and it gets worse. All the daily scores—line items per man hour and measurement tons—were compiled into a document called the Uniform Management Report. It was expensive to run, too heavy for a man to lift, and evidently very difficult to understand. A top manager told me he never looked at the thing, which was fine, since the numbers that went into it were garbage anyway.

Nothing drives a Quality Age firm forward like valid, useful scorekeeping, and it's up to management to insist on it and then use it.

I've devoted this chapter to management, and we've covered a lot of ground. I think what it all comes down to is *taking responsibility* and *open, honest, fruitful communication.*

Dr. Deming lays the blame for stagnation on "the failure of managers to manage."[11]

That's true. Through the steps I've described here, management will be able to create working environments that encourage communication, allow flexibility, and actively and positively deal with change.

5

The Quality Work Force

In 1968, I landed a summer job sweeping floors in a huge Midwestern soap plant. It wasn't glamorous, but it had its advantages. For one thing, it paid $3.47 an hour, money I badly needed for college. For another thing, there was little danger of becoming a fatality, so I was already way ahead of the summer of '67.

The first day on the job, I plunged into work with something close to gusto. At 10 o'clock, one of my co-workers breezed by me. "Break time, Perry," he called.

My broom didn't stop. "No, thanks. I'm not tired."

I swept on, like a madman. Lunch time came. I knocked off work and grabbed a sandwich with the other men. Just half an hour later, I cleaned up. "Time to head back," I said.

"Where? To work?" one of them said, echoing the laughter of the others. "Come on, sit down, take it easy."

"Really," I said, "I've had my half hour. Besides, there's a lot to do out there. I'll never get it done today if I don't hustle."

They weren't laughing now. "Today?" one of them asked. "Perry, you can't get that done today. That's a week's worth of work out there."

"Aw heck no!" I said. "I can get it done. Just have to keep moving." I left them and went back to work.

The next morning, during break period, several co-workers walked over to my area to find me hard at work. "Break time, Perry," one of them noted.

"Thanks," I said, "but I'm not tired."

"Doesn't look good for you to work that hard," one of them said.

"I've got to get this done." I answered.

They grumbled and moved on. I took my 30 minute lunch, skipped the afternoon break, and was hard at it early the next morning when a larger group of men surrounded me. If I hadn't been so sure it was a group, I might have suspected it was a mob.

"You don't get the picture, Perry," one of them began.

"This is a week's worth of work here, easy," another chimed in.

"You're messing up," someone else said.

"You're killing the rate," someone grumbled.

"Better get the message."

"Better learn your lesson."

"Look, guys," I said, getting a little hot. "I've got a job to do here. The boss gave it to me to do, and I'm going to do it. I'm minding my own business; now how about you just mind yours?"

They drifted away, and I heard no more about it.

The following Monday, out of the clear blue, I was summoned to the personnel office. I was told, without explanation that I'd been transferred. My new job? Shoveling rancid vegetable fat that had accumulated over a year's time into a gigantic vat.

The work looked as vile and disgusting as you might imagine. But what could I do? I started to work. I lifted my first shovelful, caught a whiff of the awful stuff, dropped the shovel, and threw up.

My new foreman was watching from a safe distance. He called, "Don't worry, you'll get used to it."

"Great," I wheezed. My eyes had fogged up. I wiped them, then gamely picked up the shovel and pressed on.

I shoveled the shift away and trudged out of the vat, dizzy and drained and definitely disheartened. One of my former colleagues fell into step with me. "Howya like the new job, Perry?"

All I could do was shake my head.

"Better than sweeping floors?" he jibed.

My look at him could have burned holes through granite.

"Betcha been thinking about that sweeping job a lot," he mused. "Whaddya think? Still think you can get it all done in one day?"

"Huh?"

"Listen up," he said impatiently. "You still feel like you should work through breaks and stuff?"

I began to see the light. "Oh no," I said. "Breaks are important. You get tired; you need your rest."

"What about lunch breaks?"

"An hour. A full hour," I enthused. "You need time for your meal to digest." Digestion was very much on my mind at the time.

"What about the job itself?" he prompted. "How long does it take to finish? A day or a week?"

"Oh, a week, definitely," I nodded vigorously. "No question about it. A week is what it takes. A whole entire week, yes sir."

"Well, I don't know. There's been talk lately about how maybe that job can be done in just one day," he said doubtfully.

"What are you talking about?" I asked, indignant. "A *day* to do that job? Ridiculous. It takes a week, easy."

The next week I was out of the vat and back behind the broom. I'd learned my lesson.

This kind of thing is common in stagnant firms—organized lassitude, an atmosphere of paranoia and withdrawal, and resentment and coercion of anyone who dares to "break the rate." Typically, the management of a stagnant firm will use this as an alibi for poor results. Some go so far as to cite it as evidence of the "decline of the American worker," to which I say: Hogwash.

There have always been, and will always be, bad apples in any particular bunch. You don't have to be a statistician to know that. But I vehemently reject the idea that American workers as a group have declined. In fact, I think American workers are better than they've ever been. They're still the best in the world. What has declined is management.

We've already discussed how management of stagnant firms has lost touch with customer expectations, focused on secondary goals, and sponsored supplier relations that are down-right destructive. As damaging as all that is, an even bigger problem is management's failure to take *the cultural characteristics of American workers* into account.

Today's American workers bear the cultural stamp of their immigrant forebears: rebellious, proud, free-thinking, individualistic, and intensely competitive. But stagnant management treats workers as replaceable parts with all the individualism of plant and equipment. Management in these firms is a never-ending effort to force lockstep conformity upon people who, from the earliest days of childhood, were taught that they are special and unique.

It's been suggested that we can all improve by emulating the Japanese. Certainly there's a lot to learn from them. But we'd sell them short by saying that their "worker uniformity" management style is the unquestionable ideal. What the Japanese do is manage in a way that capitalizes on their workers' cultural heritage.

That's how America's Quality Age firms operate, too. They manage workers in a way that capitalizes on our own cultural heritage, which is quite different from that of the Japanese. They manage American workers in light of what they are: proud, competitive individuals.

A New Mindset

The goal of the activities I'll describe in this chapter is to effect a *total philosophy change* among workers—to change their mindset. Stagnant firms have the pervasive attitude that "we don't want to get any better." Goals are set and clung to for dear life. No one ever wants to do any better than that prescribed, "safe" range. Frequently, students at my seminars tell me that it's almost a publicized corporate goal never to improve. I think that's out of fear, because improvement means change.

We want to replace that mindset with a whole new attitude, a whole new thinking process. We want workers to *think about what they're doing.* More important, we want them to ask constant, probing questions: "How are we doing? How much better are we doing today than yesterday? What can we do to improve even more?"

Through effective scorekeeping, we'll learn once and for all how good (or how bad) we're doing. We'll face our situation honestly and encourage that same honesty in our workers. When top managers set the example and accept the straight facts without rancor, workers will begin to level with them and level with each other without fear of punishment.

Then we will create an atmosphere and a structure, a network, with which everyone will work together to improve. This will begin to dissipate the pervasive air of defeatism that permeates stagnant operations. The general feeling should be one of acceptance and determination. We're not losers, we're winners; all we have to do now is prove it. We're not looking for overnight success. All we want and expect is for everything to get just a little bit better every day.

It's a phenomenal change from the worker environment that exists in stagnant firms. But it can be done. Our many Quality Age firms prove it every day. The starting place is the total commitment of top management that we discussed in the last chapter. This is buttressed by the management practices I described.

At the same time, we put into place a series of activities designed to help create the quality workforce.

Winning the Workforce Over

I've been in the quality and productivity improvement business for a long time. I've seen many mistakes made, and I've made quite a few myself. And one of the worst mistakes made in the improvement effort is in the way the program is presented to the work force.

Often, it's not presented; it's dictated: thrown at the workers, stuffed down their throats. Often, the program consists of a pep talk and some intense training and then, *bang!* Everything's supposed to get better, magically. We just can't handle it this way. Not if we want our improvement program to become autonomous and self-sustaining.

Essentially, managers have to accept the fact that they can't dictate the program to the work force. The work force has to be sold on the program—wooed, so to speak. It's analogous to an effort to sell a major product to a major customer, a sales effort that means life or death to the firm.

This sales effort—for that's what it is, in the most constructive sense of the term—should have, as its starting point, an appreciation of how the workers feel about things at the present moment.

Put yourself in their place. First off, consider basic human nature. People hate and dread change. That includes your people. The mere idea of an improvement program sends shock waves of dread through the work force. It's not the program per se; it's the fact of change itself. I could announce a company-paid party every day, and some people would resist, as they would resist anything new, anything novel, anything that disturbs the status quo.

Oddly enough, the majority of the work force generally *hates* the status quo. They think it stinks and gripe about it endlessly. Yet they'll rush to its defense and guard it with their lives at the approach of anything that threatens to disturb it.

Add to that syndrome the feelings of skepticism and contempt that tend to pervade the stagnant firm's work force. Most firms with which I've worked with have attempted various types of improvement programs before. Some have gone through many different iterations, all with the same result: everything gradually goes back to the way it's always been. This is not lost on the work force; there's a lot of scoffing at management's latest brainchild as well as in response to even the most earnest promises to "turn over a new leaf."

Then there is the entire litany of more specific objections that inevitably bubble to the surface:

- *"They want to get more work out of us."* This is always the first assumption. Workers in stagnant firms tend to believe that management has ulterior motives, always at the expense of workers.

- *"They want to eliminate jobs."*   This is another supposed ulterior motive that is especially indicative of a forbidding wall between management and the work force.

- *"Now they want to make inspectors out of us."* In most firms, those with inspection responsibility are paid more than general hourly workers; this is a version of the "more work for less money" fear.

- *"Statistics! Oh God, I hate statistics!"* As word of the new scorekeeping systems get around, workers—who have probably not been in school for a decade or more—hark back to their classroom days and recall that their most hated and dreaded subject was math. They remember how boring and awful the teachers were, how stupid they felt. Now management is pushing their faces right back into it! More than once, workers have said to me: "If we were cut out to be statisticians, do you think we'd be dumb enough to work here?"

That's the environment with which you're starting. As you can see, marching the work force into the program virtually at gunpoint is not likely to succeed all that well. We have to win them over first—at least to the point where they're willing to listen. Till you've got their interest and attention, all the talk in the world is worthless.

Through many trials and much error, I've developed a way to get the attention and the sincere interest of the work force. It's a kind of informal presentation that I make to them. In it I address the following general topics:

- *"How many of you would like to make more money?"* That's question number one, and I guarantee you it gets their attention right away. After all, who *doesn't* want to make more money? In fact, after asking that question I inform the group that anyone who is happy with his or her income, who doesn't want to make any more money, is excused. No one leaves.

- *Talking turkey.* I begin with the premise that workers have a pretty good idea of what tough shape the firm is in. But even so I give it to them straight. I talk about the competition, domestic and foreign. I tell the workers straight out that these competitive pressures will inevitably smother the firm to death unless changes are made.

Then I get back to their natural desire to make money. The question is: From where is this money to come? The firm doesn't have it to give, in the current state of things. The workers can make protests, issue demands, go out on strike, or anything else—the firm just can't pay more. If these tactics persist, the firm's only option will be the one the steel companies used—closing facilities down.

I talk about the pattern of today's firms: The strong are getting stronger, the weak are getting weaker and will eventually disappear. This is the natural, if unfortunate, fate of firms that do not make changes and improve.

- *The path to recovery.* I tell them straight out that the only way the firm can generate more money for its workers is to improve the quality of its products and services—to restore and improve competitive position—and to improve productivity. If we do that, we'll get more business, which will allow us not only to save existing jobs, but also to hire more people and to expand.

  I tell them that is the firm's goal and that management is irrevocably committed to it. The firm wants to survive and to grow.

- *The need for worker involvement.* I describe the program in some detail, but I stress the central issue of *worker involvement and responsibility.* Workers know better than anyone else what is going on in the operation at its most critical points. The problems that come out into the open may surprise management, but they won't be any startling revelations to the workers.

  Hourly personnel must have more responsibility for making decisions and for dealing with change and with improvement. The training and implementation of Integrated Quality Management will give them that responsibility.

- *Cutting manpower?* This is obviously a very sensitive issue, and I believe in addressing it with total honesty. There is no way the firm can promise that there won't be a need to cut manpower. Given the volatility of the business world, no company can legitimately make that blanket promise. Even in Japan, where much is made of the "life-time employment" concept, permanent lifetime employment is by no means universal.

I accentuate the positive by restating the goal of the firm: to improve quality and productivity to the extent that the firm will grow and add jobs. Integrated Quality Management can make that possible. Without it, there is definitely no job security.

- *A sincere desire for their help.* I tell the hourly personnel that they are the key to the success or the failure of the improvement program. Management is committed to putting the training, the resources, and the new levels of authority in their hands, but management needs their help to make improvement happen.

I don't for a minute suggest that this type of discussion always sends workers singing back to their workstations. But it does, if delivered with genuine sincerity, honesty, and openness, create an attitude of open-mindedness among them. They may still be wary and skeptical, but when they see clearly that the issue is survival and that management is prepared to "put its money where its mouth is," they'll start to go along.

In addition, the discussion of the domestic and foreign threats to the survival of the firm begins to ignite the *competitive spirit* that is so important to the success of the program.

The Union Factor

There's little difference when the work force is composed of union members, except that their reluctance and hostility tends to be much more focused and disciplined. I remember the time I was called into do quality and productivity training at a manufacturing plant on the East Coast. I arrived on schedule to find that the workers were, at the request of the union, boycotting my training classes. The union was just flat-out opposed to the whole program, and management was wringing its hands helplessly.

But I did win them over. Here's how: I arranged a meeting of top and middle management and invited union officials to attend. In that meeting, I gave an analysis of the firm's problems and dismal prospects, placing the responsibility for the problems on *management* without mincing words.

I went on the describe the general framework of Integrated Quality Management. I stressed the need for worker involvement in and responsibility for decision making and challenged management to promise that role for them.

Well, all of this was music to the union officials' ears. It confirmed what they'd been saying for years: that the workers could help fix quality and productivity problems if only management would let them. I went on to conduct my training seminars, which went off without a hitch. Today that plant is one of the most productive and efficient of all the firms with which I've worked.

Ultimately, I have found that, of all employee functions and levels, the hourly work force ends up being the most receptive and positive about the improvement program. But we have to deal with absolute openness, honesty, and sincerity—and we have to follow through with what we promise.

Once we have laid the groundwork by getting the workers' sincere interest and attention, we can proceed to other phases of Integrated Quality Management such as developing scorekeeping systems and conducting training.

But at the same time there are other things we must do in developing our quality workforce.

Feedback Programs

Suggestion boxes are certainly nothing new. Firms have used them for years, and many are thrilled to get as many as one suggestion for every two employees per year. In Japan, the volume of suggestions has exceeded *nine per employee per year*. Quite a difference!

Why the spread? Suggestion programs are effective only to the extent that management acknowledges and acts upon the suggestions, and recognizes and rewards those that make them. As I've said repeatedly, the work force consists of a staggering amount of thought, intelligence, and ability. It's like the Quality Image in that it is the typical firm's most undervalued and underrecognized resource.

With action, response, and encouragement, we can tap that fund of intelligence with remarkable results.

Teams

Ask any baseball fan what major league team constantly has the greatest number of superstar players. The answer will, invariably, be the New York Yankees. Yet when did the Yankees last win a pennant? 1981. The World Series? 1978. In fact, in the era of Yankee owner George Steinbrenner—a man whose exuberance for acquiring the superstar of the moment (at any cost) is near-legendary—the Yankees have won the World Series exactly twice, and not at all in the 1980s. Three other teams, possessed of considerably less player reputation, have done at least as well.

In baseball, the team's the thing, not the players. The same is true in business. Without communication, joint effort, and the team spirit, no one wins. Yet what I see in so many stagnant firms is a collection of individuals who not only don't work together, but actively oppose each other.

For example, back in my auto industry days, I was having a problem with one of my Big Three customers. In order to resolve the problem, I needed to meet with the firm's purchasing and engineering people. The simplest thing, I thought in my naiveté, was to sit down and meet with both groups at once.

Wrong. When I got there, I found I had to meet with the purchasing group and the engineering group separately. Why? They refused to get together in the same room! They all worked for the same company. Their individual and collective success depended on the success of the company. Yet the two groups regarded each other with suspicion and rivalry. You'd almost think they were the bitterest of competitors!

There is no such rivalry within Quality Age firms. They avoid it by instituting one or more *teams* composed of individuals from each function of the process. Each individual, in turn, represents a team of those who work in each individual function.

These cross-functional teams recognize the fact that every firm consists of a network of interdependencies. The workers in each function, as I've said, are the customers of the workers in the previous function, and suppliers to those of the next one. It's not enough to tell people performing one "You give this to the people in the next function," expressed as some sort of target; change and variation always come into play and must be dealt with.

I recommend that the cross-functional teams meet at least once per month. Such team meetings are, of course, not a new idea; quality circles, organized along functional lines, have been used in American firms for many years.

But there are problems with the way many of today's quality circles are handled. In my observation, they tend to lack direction and focus. They seem to be meetings for the sake of having meetings. Even worse, they sometimes turn into gripe sessions: us versus them; workers versus management. People complain about the locations of the water coolers, the quality of the lighting in the facility, the roughness of the toilet paper; you name it.

In Quality Age firms, team meetings, quality circles, and the like are focused on the issues that are important to the overall goals of the firm. Whether a team is composed of people working in an identical function in the process or people representing each function in the process, the general topics for discussion are:

- What effect does our work have on meeting the customer goal?
- How good is the work we're doing compared with the goals that we have set for ourselves?
- What are the ways that we can do better?

- Are there system changes that need to be made so that we can improve?

For example, a team of warehouse stock pickers may be getting inaccurate picking slips from the computer room. In their own team meeting, they can discuss this problem and look for ways to solve it themselves. If they can't solve it themselves, then their representative brings it up in the meeting of the team that includes all the other process functions in the warehouse. In this case, the stock pickers are the "customers" of the computer room and are receiving bad "supply."

With the advice and counsel of the other functional reps, the computer room rep and the stock picker rep can explore the problem and identify ways to solve it. The solution may be something they can implement themselves, or it may require a system change that needs to be brought to management's attention.

In any case, the burden for solving the problem now falls quite naturally on the workers themselves. It isn't just tossed into management's lap. It doesn't need to go to management at all unless it's a system problem. It's dealt with early, not after it's gotten out of hand.

And it's dealt with in a positive, constructive way. Under the old, stagnant system of isolation, stock pickers might grumble about the bad picking tickets, complain about "those bozos in the computer room." Animosity might develop, the situation might deteriorate, and by the time management got involved, the problem might have become extreme with battle lines drawn between the opposing camps, all pointing fingers at one another.

Under the stagnant system, workers had the knowledge to solve many of the daily, running problems themselves, but no power. Under the Quality Age system, the workers have the power and the unequivocal backing of management. The burden shifts from management to workers. This makes individual workers feel important, respected, and valued. It restores pride and self-respect.

The team system helps unite the operation as a whole, causes it to act in a coordinated way, like a well-disciplined orchestra. The team system also helps recreate the entrepreneurial atmosphere even within our largest firms.

Part of the stagnation syndrome is, undeniably, a function of growth. Individuals and individual effort and initiative get lost in the masses. Teams, when properly constituted and effectively run, become in effect small, entrepreneurial business entities within the larger firm.

Several factors are essential to effective team activities:

- *Short, to-the-point meetings.* Team meetings must never become ends in themselves. I see no reason that any team meeting should last more than one hour. To keep the time within bounds, there should be a facilitator for each team (this responsibility can rotate) who in fact coordinates and does not direct. The facilitator maintains a kind of brief agenda by which the meetings are run to keep the discussion on track and to follow through on results. A one-hour time limit—I've implemented some with 30-minute time limits—creates a sense of urgency and keeps the meetings from wandering all over the map.

- *Brainstorming.* The most effective team meetings, while conducted briskly and efficiently, also permit brainstorming. This means we have to have a positive and receptive atmosphere, and we have to allow some time for the discussion of ideas, no matter how "off-the-wall" they may sound at first. Most real breakthroughs originate as an idea germinating in someone's head, and we have to give those ideas room. Of course, many will be proven impractical after they've been brought out and discussed, but that's all right. *Quantity* of ideas is vital.

- *The Quality Image.* An essential recurring topic in team activities must be the Quality Image. This is, as I've stressed a concern of everyone, not just top management. Each team should be aware of the ways in which its activities affect the Quality Image, and every prospective change must be evaluated in light of its potential effect on the Quality Image.

- *Scorekeeping.* Scorekeeping systems and results are central to the effectiveness of teams and team meetings. How we're doing today, as measured by our scorekeeping, is always a hot topic. If we're doing worse, why? If we're doing better, why? If we did this, what would be the effect on our score? What can we do to make today's score just a little bit better than yesterday's?

Making Work a Game

Is any society in the world as competitive as the American society? I don't think so. Americans are competitive through and through. An obvious example is the overwhelming popularity of spectator sports of all kinds. We even love vicarious competition: baseball, football, basketball, and hockey; professional sports; college sports; and the Olympics. These events enjoy various levels of popularity worldwide, but nowhere as much as right here. And where else is automobile racing or marathon running so popular, to the extent that such events draw big ratings on TV?

Americans of all walks of life participate in various sporting activities too. Where else do people put in a long working day, then change clothes and play softball or handball or golf for hours? Sure, we do it partly out of concern for physical fitness. Some of us do it as a social outlet or to develop business and professional contacts. But I think we do it more to feed our appetites for competition.

Nonphysical competition is as prevalent as physical. Many Americans compete with board games, card games, word games; you name it. And organized competition is only half the story. We compete for status. We compete for income. We compete with our siblings, our peers, and society at large. We compete with and through our children. At the back of our minds is the continuous questioning: "How am I doing? How are they doing? Where do I stack up? What can I do to get ahead?"

The appetite for competition is a major component of the American psyche, a reflection of our origins as a society. It's a force that Quality Age firms draw upon with positive results. They use competition to bring a sense of fun to people's work.

The most productive and efficient people are those who enjoy their work, those who are lucky enough to have found their "calling," work that they not only enjoy but get paid to do. To them, the job is not really work; it's something they want to do and enjoy doing.

A large number of people, certainly a majority of workers, do not fall into this category. Most wind up in jobs or professions that are, in some sense, the least intolerable of all the options open to them. To them, work is not fun, or a game. It's in some sense a necessary evil, something to be endured and dispensed with. This is not their fault; it's the way things are. You can't expect them to bring to the job an abundance of zest, a feeling of anticipation, a sense of fun. Instead, we have to create that sense of fun. We do it through competition: by making work a game through our new team structure.

In some forms, this kind of competition is obvious and widely practiced. Sales teams can and do compete with one another. They compete for the highest sales, for the largest number of new customers, for the highest level of repeat business.

But that's only one form of competition, and it applies to but one segment of our entire process. There's another way to create positive competition that can involve literally *every* team in the firm. I call it *the improvement game*.

Quite simply, teams compete to see who can achieve the highest level of improvement in a given period. Of course, each team out of necessity has to define improvement differently. A sales team, for example, can define improvement as "more sales this period than last period." A production team, on the other hand, may define improvement as "less tolerance variation this period than last period" or "more productivity this period than last."

Through effective scorekeeping, both of these teams can be put on a level playing field, allowing them to compete with each other. The concept is like handicapping in golf; in this scenerio, competition is based not on actual results but on *rate of improvement.*

The specific numbers—total sales, number of defects, whatever—aren't so important; what matters is the comparative rate at which things improve.

When you view the situation this way, the horizon of potential games and competition expands dramatically. And the results of this kind of competitive, game-playing structure can be tremendous. Competition brings a sense of excitement to the workplace. It ignites workers' enthusiasm. It creates peer pressure, unifying teams in a way nothing else can. It brings a sense of play to activities that workers previously regarded as sheer drudgery.

Suddenly, work doesn't feel quite so much like work. Employees are motivated in a way they have never been before. Production and quality go up. Absenteeism and turnover go down. Workers do much less clockwatching and "living for the weekend."

Tom Monaghan of Domino's Pizza gives us a sense of the dynamism and excitement that the "game of doing well" can bring to an operation:

> [The real beauty of our system] is in the thrill of working as a team when the pace gets really frantic, when the phones are ringing without letup and the drivers are running back out the door right after they come in. People respond to that kind of challenge. It's a game, and the ones who have a knack for it can go a long way at Domino's.[12]

Rewards and Incentives

Quality Age firms motivate by creating positive competition among teams. Just the satisfaction of having done well and better than before is a form of reward and can raise productivity and quality to new levels.

But the impact of competition and games is heightened when the winners receive various forms of rewards and incentives. You see this kind of thing in various places, usually in the context of sales: bonuses, incentives, commissions, prizes of various kinds.

But just as I see competition as a spark that can ignite the whole firm—not just the sales end—I see a rewards-and-incentives system as something that can be creatively applied to the whole firm.

And "reward" doesn't necessarily and automatically have to mean money. A major, and often overlooked, form of reward is something I've touched on before: *recognition*. Seek out victories, and publicize the victors. This taps another key component of the American psyche: the uniqueness of the individual. We all think of ourselves as special; we want to be recognized as individuals.

In the Quality Age firm, there are two effective elements to the *recognition* form of award.

- *Recognition is weighted toward the "lower" ranks of the firm.* With the team system, most ideas and solutions will emanate from the lower ranks anyway; it's essential that they—not the managers responsible for them—get the credit. Patting a manager on the back for an idea or a solution that actually came from a team or an individual further down is, I guarantee you, an instant turn-off.

- *Recognition of the achievement is universally publicized within the firm.* It's particularly important that every one of the recipient's peers be aware of it. Quality Age firms even look for ways to publicize the achievement outside the firm.

One ideal vehicle for this recognition is a company newsletter distributed to all hands. The newsletter item should include a description of the achievement as well as some personal details about the achiever. Another popular forum is a group meeting or a ceremony of some kind during which the achiever is personally recognized.

Quality Age firms make *recognition* a principal component of every reward system—and there's more. They take steps to promote the *status* of achievers. Things such as individualized plaques and reserved parking spaces bearing the person's name can work very well. So do extra days off with pay.

I've found that cash incentives, while effective, are not necessarily the most effective form of rewards. They don't have the same positive psychological effect of personal recognition and enhanced status.

Some firms are reluctant to employ these kinds of incentives. They seem to feel that such incentives are ineffective simply because they don't cost much. They think an incentive has to be *money* or it won't work. That's not true, and I have an example to prove it.

One particular client had a cash bonus incentive system, of sorts. Achievers won a $25 bonus from which taxes were deducted in advance, making the net bonus about $17. Because of the length of time it took to process all the paperwork, the money wasn't paid till six or nine months later. Over half the recipients handed the checks back!

Then, after I'd worked with this firm for a while, management decided on a different type of reward. This was to be an expenses-paid party for the group of achievers. Unfortunately, the firm allocated very little money from its budget for this party. So the achievers were treated to sugarless Kool-Aid and six-cent hot dogs in day-old buns. You know what? The workers were thrilled.

It is indeed amazing what competition, reward, and incentive systems can do, even if they don't cost much.

In my own firm, we have periods when employees embroiled in our contests begin coming in earlier and earlier to get the jump on others. Sometimes they stay so late we have to kick them out at the end of the day!

Quality Age firms tie all of this together with scorekeeping systems that are fair and objective—systems the workers believe in. Effective scorekeeping is central to Integrated Quality Management, as I've stressed over and over in this book. Now let's talk about scorekeeping.

PART III

QUALITY TOOLS AND TECHNIQUES

You're familiar with the scenario; you've seen it a million times in movies and on TV. Perhaps you've even participated in it yourself.

Moments before the start of a football game, the coach gathers the players together in the locker room, and he gives them a talk. The styles vary. Some coaches mimic General Patton, vowing destruction to the enemy. Some coaches go a little nuts, yelling and screaming and throwing things around the room. Others go just the opposite direction, speaking in a calm, low, rational voice.

Whatever the style, the purpose of this pregame talk is to get the players' attention, cause them to focus on the challenge ahead, motivate them, pump them up.

When this pep talk is done correctly, the players come charging out of the locker room, mentally prepared. They know that their mission is to win. They bring a sense of purpose to their game.

But is that all they bring with them? Certainly not. If that were all, their efforts would be pretty hopeless. They also bring with them knowledge of the rules of the game. And, most critically, they bring with them detailed knowledge of the plays they're going to execute. They've been over that play book a million times, put in hundreds of hours of practice, so that their movements are practically second nature.

Often, in our improvement efforts, we deliver the same sort of pump-'em-up pep talks. These are certainly important, but, as I've said, there's a lot more to improvement than pep talks. Unless we do more, the workers charge out of the "locker room" and back to the same old workplace, facing the same old problems and frustrations.

Quality Age firms rely on more than just motivation. Just as football players need rules and plays to make them successful, Quality Age workers need tools and techniques—which, in the language of improvement, means scorekeeping.

6

The Great Scorekeeper

It was Game One of the 1988 World Series, bottom of the ninth, two outs, one man on. Los Angeles Dodgers manager Tommy Lasorda decided to send a pinch-hitter to the plate to face Oakland's ace reliever Dennis Eckersley.

The player Lasorda chose was Kirk Gibson, a slugger who had not started the game due to injured legs. Despite that, Gibson cranked a pitch over the right-field fence.

Why did Dodgers fans go nuts? Why did this one at-bat in the first World Series game guarantee Gibson hero status? What made this event one of the most dramatic in recent sports history? The answers to those questions lie in a key piece of information that I've withheld so far.

The score, as Gibson limped to the plate, was Oakland 3, Los Angeles 2.

Gibson's two-run homer snatched victory for the Dodgers from the jaws of defeat. It erased Oakland's home-field advantage and paved the way for the Dodgers' World Series triumph in five games.

There's no drama, no excitement, no enjoyment to any sport unless you know the score. There's no point to it, either. No one will watch nine innings of baseball, 48 minutes of basketball, or 60 minutes of football or hockey without knowing the score.

But the score is only part of the story. Behind it is a myriad of other scores, measurements, and statistics. These are central to every manager's strategy. Baseball in particular has become riddled with statistics, far beyond the traditional batting and earned run averages. For example, managers consider pitching performance on natural versus artificial turf, slugging percentage, and batting average with men in scoring position. And as each new statistic comes along, fans gobble it up.

So I always have to smile a little bit when people come up to me in plants and at seminars all shaken up at the idea of keeping score with statistical methods. The comments go something like this: "My people hate math! They hate statistics! We can't make them do this stuff; they just barely got through high school!" And so on.

Well, the fact is that everyone—from hourly laborer up to chief executive officer—uses measurement, scorekeeping, and *statistics* in daily life. No one gives it a second thought.

As I've pointed out, scorekeeping and statistics not only enhance the enjoyment of sports, they actually create it. But another area of daily life in which statistics plays a vital role is personal finances.

Virtually everyone has a checking account. This is nothing more than a simple, yet useful statistical system. It helps us govern our finances, see where we are at any given time.

Most of us stay aware, to the penny, of how much money we have at any point. When our balance gets low, we make a deposit. We don't wait for checks to bounce before getting around to depositing money. The statistical system helps us make decisions, tells us when it's time to do certain things.

Statistics also plays a vital role in the financial operations of our firms. You wouldn't dream of running a firm without balancing your checking accounts, for one thing. And accounting systems are almost universally used to let owners and managers see what's going on, to help them keep score.

Statistics and scorekeeping are, then, integral to most forms of human activity. They are also unquestionably vital in the management of corporate finances.

Why, then, don't stagnant firms practice scientific scorekeeping in other areas of the operation? Actually, they make all kinds of attempts to measure and keep score in various areas. The problem is that their methods tend to be unscientific, nonobjective. Here are some examples of what I mean.

How Many "Good" Bumpers?

Back in my automotive days, I ran an operation that made
polyurethane bumpers. Once, during a crunch, I got a call to
ship 2,500 bumpers right away. As it happened, I had 2,500
bumpers in inventory. But there was one problem. Rick, one
of my directors, said he couldn't ship them. They were all bad.

"What's so bad about them?" I asked.

"They're scratched, Perry," he told me. "Lots of scratches.
Big ones. We can't ship them out."

Well, I was under the gun. I had to get at least some
bumpers out the door yesterday. I called in Bob, a foreman,
and explained the problem to him.

"Here's the thing," I said. "You know how Rick is. Real
picky sometimes. He said all 2,500 bumpers are bad, but I can't
believe that all of them are *really* that bad. Go on over, take a
look at them, see how many are really that bad. See if we can
salvage some."

Bob did as I asked and came back with his report. "You're
right, Perry. Only about half of them are really bad. We can
ship the other 1,200."

That helped, but I still had the problem. The plant needed
2,500 and wouldn't take no for an answer. But I couldn't ship
out bad ones. I called in Mary, one of the supervisors, and
explained the problem to her.

"Here's the thing," I said. "You know how Bob is. Real picky
sometimes. He said all 1,200 of these bumpers are bad, but I
can't believe that all of them are *really* that bad. Go on over,
take a look at them, see how many are really that bad. See if
we can salvage some."

Mary did as I asked and came back with her report. "You're
right, Perry. Only about half of them are really bad. We can
ship the other 600. "

I seemed to be on a roll now. I fended off another demanding call from manufacturing, then sent for Dave, who was a
foreman. I explained the problem to him.

"Here's the thing," I said. "You know how Mary is. Real
picky sometimes. She said all 600 of these bumpers are bad,
but I can't believe that all of them are *really* that bad. Go on

over, take a look at them, see how many are really that bad. See if we can salvage some."

Dave did as I asked and came back with his report. "You're right, Perry. Only about half of them are really bad. We can ship the other 300."

It was getting to be really funny. Each person I sent found that half of what they inspected was, in fact, good. If I kept on this way, I'd find I had 150 bad, then 75 bad, 37, 18, 9, 4, 2, 1. Why go through all that? Why not ship them all out now?

So we did.

The Calipers

I can't tell you how many times I've seen people using calipers to measure things to the nearest 10,000th of an inch. The problem is that calipers won't measure that finely. Often, too, I've found that, when calipers are used by strong men, no part is ever too big. They can always squeeze them down tight enough to get the measurement they want.

The biggest laugher of all was the time I had a worker measuring some different parts with a caliper, and he kept getting a reading of 385. Every single part was 385 thick. It turned out he was reading the caliper's model number.

A New Form of Random Sampling

While developing the improvement program at that West Coast warehouse/distribution operation, I learned that they had a rather interesting approach to random sampling for warehouse inspections.

Normally, random sampling is just that. You go in, choose items purely at random, and count them. But that wasn't the case at this firm. There, inspectors were told, in advance, what they could sample. They were specifically excluded from sampling among any warehoused items that weren't on the list.

There's no question about it: the scorekeeping techniques within stagnant firms tend to be flawed, capricious, and ultimately meaningless. Quality Age firms, on the other hand, practice objective, valid scorekeeping in the key areas of the process—not just manufacturing. They regard it as the single most critical thing they can do to effect never-ending improvement.

- I talked about how important honesty is—facing the truth, knowing what's going on. Scorekeeping helps us to do that. Scorekeeping helps us face reality, communicate it, and deal with it.

- To be able to deliver customer satisfaction, we have to know what we can really do, what our process is *capable* of doing. Scorekeeping helps us learn that.

- I've talked at length about ways to get workers involved. Scorekeeping helps us to do that because the scorekeeping methods I'm going to describe *are administered by the workers themselves*.

- Finally, objective scorekeeping makes competition, rewards, and incentives effective.

Ultimately, *constant improvement* is what we're after. As I've pointed out, achieving this requires many changes in the way we do things, both within the firm and outside it. At the bottom of it all is a fair, objective scorekeeping system.

SPC: The Great Scorekeeper

Several times I've talked about *variation*, the fact that no two things are ever exactly the same and no two activities are ever performed exactly the same way with identical results. Variation is a fact of life. It is present in every repetitive activity. We all know that.

Bowling, for example, is an extremely repetitive activity. The bowler rolls each ball with but one intent: to knock down all the standing pins. Though the bowler's goal is very focused, and the actions she takes to achieve that goal are very limited, the results constantly *vary*, don't they? In five games the bowler may score 179, 183, 205, 195, 190. No one gives that a second thought. But scores of 193, 193, 193, 193, and 193 would cause quite a stir.

Actually, there are two kinds of variation. *Normal variation* (sometimes called "chance" or "random" variation) is a purely natural phenomenon. It's a variation that cannot be attributed to any specific cause. *Abnormal variation* is variation that *can* be attributed to a specific type of cause or causes.

For example, let's look at two groups of bowling scores. The first group is

179, 183, and 188

The second group is

151, 138, and 119

The first group of scores is clumped fairly close together with little variation. The second group is spread over a much wider range. Further, there is a very wide gap between the groups.

If we look at those six scores as a group and assume that the first three represent historical variability, it's clear that something happened between the third score and the fourth. Something changed. Abnormal variation intruded. We call the source of this abnormal variation *an assignable cause*.

Obviously, our goal in bowling is consistently to roll the highest scores possible. Therefore, we need to know the assignable cause for that abnormal variation so we can correct it.

One assignable cause could be a change in bowlers. A proficient bowler may have rolled the first group; a less skillful bowler the second. Or the same bowler may have rolled all six games, but tripped over someone's shoes between games 3 and 4 and wrenched her leg. Or, having chug-a-lugged a beer before the fourth game, she may not have been, shall we say, quite as sharp anymore. Or she may have switched to a lane whose floor had a warp in it. Maybe the bowler changed to a different and less comfortable ball between games 3 and 4 or decided to try for Brooklyn-style strikes rather than rolling to the right side.

Bowling is, as we said, a system of repetitive activities. A natural component of the system is *random variation*. This causes varying results and is inherent. The system is also subject to *abnormal variation*, which can cause results to vary even more. Abnormal variation is due to some *assignable cause*.

Exactly the same thing is true of businesses. Ultimately, they consist of networks of repetitive activities. We do a certain number of things over and over again, aimed at achieving a desired result. As with bowling, each of these repetitive activities is subject to normal chance variation, and each is vulnerable to abnormal variation due to assignable causes.

Making a Part

Let's say our machine shop's goal is to produce a part to within 5/1000 of an inch. In a perfect world, the maximum effect of normal variation allows the operation to function within this tolerance. But abnormal variation may intrude as a result of various assignable causes. The steel we work with may be of inconsistent thickness. The tooling may wear. Operators become tired. Electrical power may fluctuate.

Sales Performance

A particular salesperson may, over two years time, produce an average of $10,000 in sales per week, ranging between $8,000 and $12,000. If that salesperson suddenly starts averaging $8,500 a week ranging between $3,000 and $14,000, we know that abnormal variation has intruded. This could be due to any number of assignable causes, including lower-quality leads, insufficient training in new products, or inefficient clerical support.

Invoice Processing

A clerk may be expected to process around 10 invoices per hour with no errors. Abnormal variation may appear in the form of lower production and the presence of errors due to assignable causes such as computer problems, inaccurate input, or the imposition of additional duties.

Why Monitor Variation?

"So what?" you say. "I know all about what you call assignable causes. I deal with them all the time. "

Certainly we deal with them. Often it seems as if that's all we do: deal with crises and stamp out forest fires. In stagnant firms, problem solving is virtually the exclusive duty of management. There are two problems with this:

1. Of all the work groups, management is usually the least familiar with the intricacies of the system and therefore the least likely to implement solutions that work.

2. By the time a problem comes to management's attention, it has become a full-blown crisis. Fifty, sixty, seventy percent of the parts are out of spec and must be scrapped; sales performance has dropped like a stone; invoice processing is backed up to last March.

Quality Age firms know that it doesn't have to be this way. They understand variation, study variation, deal with the causes of variation. They know that

• Variation and quality are inextricably linked. Low variation does not always equal high quality. But high variation always produces low quality, even if we're aiming to deliver exactly what the customer wants.

• The health of any business system is determined by how much normal variation is present and by how resistant the system is to the causes of abnormal variation.

• Abnormal variation is the precursor of problems, especially quality problems. Monitoring variation is an early warning system that enables us to detect the beginning of abnormal variation. Once we detect the intrusion of variation, we can find the assignable cause and eliminate it well before the problems get out of hand.

Monitoring variation is the ultimate in scorekeeping—and *Statistical Process Control* (SPC) is "the great scorekeeper."

SPC: How It Works

SPC is not new; it was first developed in 1924. Though it's widely used in Japan, it was actually invented by Americans, taught to the Japanese by Americans, and is being implemented in Quality Age American firms of all kinds.

Though this technique is erroneously thought to apply solely to manufacturing, it was originally developed to track trends in the stock market and is an excellent scorekeeping tool for monitoring variation in virtually *any* repetitive activity, manufacturing or service.

I won't bore you with a scholarly presentation on the statistical theory behind SPC. Suffice it to say that, by means of a small number of simple, diligently performed calculations, you can use SPC to tell the difference between natural and abnormal variation.

Let's look at bowling again. If we take 25 bowling scores and perform some simple arithmetic with them—adding and averaging—SPC will give us a picture, which we call a *control chart*, that tells us what the natural variation of our system is. As we bowl, we continue to convert our scores into points, which we post on the control chart. When these points fall within the normal range, we know that our variation is normal. When points begin to exhibit certain patterns—such as falling outside the normal range—then we know that abnormal variation due to an assignable cause has intruded.

With a little training and some experience, we can become adept at interpreting the picture the SPC chart draws for us. We can spot the intrusion of abnormal variation *when it starts*, instead of much later when the problem has become severe and expensive. The pattern on the chart will even suggest where we should look to find the assignable cause of that abnormal variation. And, when we find the cause, we can correct it before it gets out of hand.

The causes of variation are always assignable to at least one of six major categories:

1. *Operator.* Variation often occurs when the person doing the work is tired, overworked, ill, or injured. It can also occur when another less competent operator is introduced. In our bowling example, the abnormal variation may have resulted from a change in bowlers between the third and fourth score.

2. *Material.* Variation can also occur when the quality of the products or services that the operator is using has

deteriorated. Our bowler, for instance, may have switched to a different ball.

3. *Machine.* Sometimes the equipment the operator is using causes variation. Maybe it's defective, wearing out, or not up to the job. Our bowler may have switched to a lane that has a warp in it.

4. *Method.* Maybe the procedure the operator is using is outdated; maybe it's not the right one to begin with; maybe the operator is poorly trained. Our bowler may be trying for Brooklyn hits now instead of rolling to the right side.

5. *Tooling.* This is a purely manufacturing-oriented cause. Perhaps tooling wear is causing the increased levels of variation that we're seeing on the charts.

6. *Environment.* This takes into account factors such as noise level, excessive heat and cold, air pollution, and physical layout of the work area.

SPC, in essence, compares current performance with past performance. It tells us in unarguable terms how we're doing. Are we doing better? Are we doing worse? If so, why? What are the trends? This naturally involves statistics, but one of the greatest things about SPC is that the statistical part is ridiculously simple. It's as simple as adding five numbers and finding the average. That's about it.

Even average hourly workers with high school educations that ended years ago can master statistics like these in short order. This is essential because these very people must be at the heart of the SPC program. They're the scorekeepers: keeping score of the process, keeping score on themselves.

Where to Use SPC

As I've said, SPC is nothing new. Many people in business are aware that it is in virtually universal use in Japan as well as in many Quality Age firms in the United States. They know how powerful it is. Yet nearly every day, it seems, someone at one of my seminars or at a client site says to me, "Yeah, SPC is great, but it will never work here. Our process is unique."

Well, of course your process, your system, your firm itself is unique. You should be glad for that; if it weren't unique, you wouldn't have a business. But that doesn't mean that SPC isn't for you. I guarantee you, no matter how unique your process or system is in general, there exists within it a large number of repetitive activities, and SPC is designed to *keep score of and monitor variation in any repetitive activity.*

Today, SPC is most commonly used in the manufacturing arena. In this arena, parts are usually made to certain specifications, and around those specifications some degree of *tolerance* is allowed. This *tolerance* is, in effect, an "accepted" degree of variability around the specification. Even if we have the ability to make the part with less variability, we generally don't— because the *tolerance* allows us not to. When we settle for being within tolerance, however, we institutionalize mediocrity.

The other problem is that often the tolerances are difficult, if not impossible, to hit. This causes workers to make more frequent adjustments in what they are doing, which only increases variation and decreases quality.

SPC causes us to look at variation itself. Merely being "within tolerance" is no longer the goal; reducing variation itself is. SPC also enables us to look at the true capability of our process, causing us to create plans and specifications that are realistic.

SPC can also be used to monitor variation in productivity. How much are we producing today? Is this normal or abnormal? If abnormal, what does the chart tell us about possible causes? Where should we look? How can we do better?

In manufacturing, we use SPC to keep an eye on the process: to watch variation and look out for the intrusion of abnormal variation. When we find and correct the causes of abnormal variation, the quality and quantity of our work becomes more consistent and therefore better.

But as valuable as SPC is in the manufacturing arena, it can make just as profound an improvement in service and administrative functions. To repeat, it works with *any repetitive activity.* For example, you can use SPC to monitor sales productivity at the individual or group level. Instead of depending on a "gut feel" for how sales should be going, you have a chart that tells you. When the chart shows that things are

improving, you can find the causes of improvement and inten-
sify them. When the chart shows sales declining, you can find
the causes and correct them. You can even use SPC as a fore-
casting tool that will tell you, early, whether a particular person is going to make it or not.

You can use SPC in all kinds of administrative functions.
Data entry, order processing, accounting, clerical, health
care activities, and more—these are all repetitive functions.
These are all subject to performance standards of quality
and productivity. These are all measurable. And these are all
afflicted with variation, both natural and abnormal. As in manufacturing, SPC enables us to monitor variation in all these
administrative activities. It gives us a picture of the process,
displays trends, and sends vivid signals when problems are
starting to develop—at the earliest stages, when they are easy
to find and correct.

Charting Rules

I know I've made it sound as though there are a million activities you can chart. And there are. But I don't mean to suggest
that it's useful, or even desirable, to go nuts and start charting
every single thing.

I've seen that happen. I've counseled firms that had done
virtually no scorekeeping in the past and then went to just
the opposite extreme when they got into SPC. Inevitably, they
produce bundles of charts, stick them in drawers, and then
complain because they're still not improving.

Charting for its own sake is not only worthless, it's also
expensive. Charts themselves are meaningless. The critical elements are *what* you chart and *how* you use the information.
It's far better to chart one or two of the right things and make
maximum use of the information than to chart three dozen
areas and consign the charts to oblivion.

Here are some general rules on SPC charting.

Chart Early in the Process

In general, your process is a sequence of activities that has a
cumulative effect. You may start with clay at one end and, after

a series of steps, end up with a ceramic coffee cup at the other. The same is true with autos, invoice processing, or whatever. Variation also has a cumulative effect within the process. The earlier it appears, the greater its effect. In other words, its effect is not linear, but exponential, in each succeeding step of the process.

A key to improvement is to control variation *at the earliest stages of the process*, before the quality problem becomes serious. (This is why it's so important to implement close partnership relationships with your suppliers, as we discussed in Chapter 3.) Variation is actually easier to control at the early stages because less has happened. There are fewer possible causes to sort through. When you focus on later stages, there are many possible causes of variation to consider.

It's analogous to a patient who shows up at the doctor's office with bloodshot eyes, seventy-five pounds underweight, coughing and hacking and passing out every five minutes. There are so many possible causes that the doctor doesn't know where to begin. Is it cancer? Tuberculosis? Had the patient shown up earlier, at the first signs of trouble, the doctor would have had an easier time spotting the emerging problem and prescribing treatment. But now it's a little too late for the doctor to suggest that the patient clean up his lifestyle, isn't it?

The same is true in your process. Focus your SPC charting at the earliest stages, rather than the later ones.

Chart Worker-Dependent Characteristics

The characteristic you chart—a part tolerance, a chemical mix, data entry errors or whatever—should be dependent on the efforts of an individual or a group of individuals. That's because it's easier to change people and their behavior than machinery or equipment. Variation due to equipment is impossible to change without very expensive and laborious replacement or overhauls. But variation due to human performance is easier to correct. On their own, people can find ways of doing things better; you can also provide training.

This aspect of charting is most important in the manufacturing area. Service and administrative functions tend to be almost totally worker-dependent.

Chart Measurable Characteristics

When you're selecting characteristics to chart, it's important to consider how easy they are to measure and how reliable their measurements will be. After all, SPC looks at how the performance of a particular action varies over time. Any inherent error in measurement will show up as variation—indistinguishable from actual variation—which can distort your study and lead to bad decisions.

Some things lend themselves to reliable measurement more easily than others. If we're looking at sales performance, we can consider dollars, or number of orders, or whatever. But especially in manufacturing, measurement error can creep in due to *what* we're measuring and *how* we're measuring it.

A perfect example is the little story I told earlier about the scratched bumpers. The problem there was, "When is a bumper too badly scratched to ship?" This is a scorekeeping issue. Each individual who considered the problem had a different opinion. When is a scratch a scratch? How many scratches must there be before we classify the bumper as defective?

In situations like this, the measurement system has to be very carefully thought out and defined so that each person making the measurements is using the same criteria.

In the early stages of your SPC charting, I recommend that you concentrate on characteristics such as weight, thickness, or total number, that can be easily measured with reliable instruments on scales that are not subject to dispute.

If you must chart a "visual" characteristic—such as the scratches on a part—the best thing is to set up some kind of defined, arbitrary rating system—from 1 to 4, at least; preferably from 1 to 10, where 10 is the best part ever made and 1 is obvious scrap. Then it's important to perform a couple of simple statistical tests—on *repeatability* and *reproducibility*—to confirm that inherent measurement error is being kept to a minimum.

And don't overlook the obvious! By this I mean: Do the people doing the measuring have the qualifications to do it? Once I was teaching a seminar in which two of the students insisted on sitting as far front in the classroom as possible. I mean, they were sitting only a couple of feet from the black-board, their big heads blocking the view of other students, but there was no choice: they said they had to sit there.

Each one wore big thick glasses. Each one squinted as I lectured and wrote on the blackboard. Each one asked me to write bigger, and bigger, and bigger. Finally I was writing in letters a foot high and a foot wide, and they said, squinting, "Yeah, that's okay, I can make that out now." I asked them, out of curiosity, what their job was in the firm. "We're the inspectors," they told me.

Chart Factors That Are Integral to the Whole Process

Make sure that whatever you chart has a profound effect on the whole process that produces your product or service. Although, as I've said, it's important to chart early in the process, an early step doesn't necessarily have a profound impact on the outcome. When we're manufacturing something from steel, we may start by inventorying or cleaning the steel. But neither of those steps has as profound an effect on the process or the product as *drawing* the steel. This principle applies equally well to non-manufacturing activities.

What it all comes down to is this: *Be selective.* You don't have to chart everything. In fact, it's most desirable not to. When effectively used, SPC is a window to the process, a view of what the process is doing. SPC should cause everyone involved to question the process, to analyze it, to find ways to improve it. It's not just a microscopic look at every little step.

So make sure that everything you're charting has a powerful impact on the process as a whole.

The Benefits of SPC

Throughout this book so far, I've alluded to the benefits of effective scorekeeping in general and SPC in particular. Now that you're familiar with the basic workings of SPC, let's take a closer look at the benefits Quality Age firms derive from their effective SPC programs.

SPC Reduces Variation and Increases Functionality

SPC does not, of course, make things work better by itself. All SPC does is give us a window on the process and send us signals about it. If we take no action in response to those signals, nothing will change, nothing will improve, and the SPC program will be a monumental waste.

But when we do take action, consistently and effectively, we will steadily reduce variation in the performance of the steps we're charting. This will inevitably improve the function of our products or services.

Most products and services consist of a network of physical components or identifiable actions, and the quality of the whole is directly related to the ability of the individual components to function well together. The more consistent each individual element is, the better the aggregate elements work together.

SPC Teaches Process Capability

Management, especially in stagnant firms, often practices a form of wishful or even delusional thinking about what the process is capable of doing. An SPC program brings a strong dose of reality—of truth and honesty—to the table. It shows the Quality Age firm in pictorial and numerical form what the process can actually do, because it's a record of how the process has performed.

You may think your process can make a part to within 5/1000 of an inch. Your SPC charts may tell you that you can make it to within only 11/1000. You may think your invoicing operation can issue 100 invoices per day. SPC may tell you it can handle only 80.

This dose of reality is especially vital in the design or product development stage. Designers and R&D people have to know what the process is capable of doing. By telling them that, SPC helps them create designs that will actually work in production.

At some point, after the program has been at work for a while, you may hit a plateau in variation reduction when all the assignable causes have been removed and there's still some level of variation. That is natural variation, inherent in the process, and cannot be reduced further without a significant change in the system itself. This is management's job—not the workers'.

On the other side of the coin, management may be under the impression that quality can be improved only by investing huge sums in overhauling the system. An effective SPC program may demonstrate that quality can be improved tremendously just by involving the workers in the removal of assignable causes of variation within the same system and with the same equipment. A major overhaul in the system should not be considered till all assignable causes of unnatural variation have been identified and removed, and only SPC can help you to do that.

SPC Provides Historical Perspective

Because an SPC program creates a historical record of what the process can do and has done, it is a vital reference source to use in planning the development of new products and services. It is also very useful in orienting new managers, who otherwise come into the picture with very little practical idea of what their process can do.

SPC Improves Communication
within the Firm

Inevitably, the various departments and functions of the firm create specialized languages to use among themselves. SPC becomes a common language that they can use to communicate with each other.

Earlier we talked about creating supplier-customer relationships within the process. The employees at each step or function know what to expect from those at the previous one and what to deliver to those at the next. With an SPC program in place, these requirements become easy to define not just in terms of targets, but in terms of the amount of variation to expect around those targets.

SPC becomes the basis for discussion in team meetings, quality circles, and so forth. Team members therefore deal with hard facts, with reality, with the nuts and bolts of improvement.

SPC Improves Communication with Vendors

We devoted Chapter 3 to describing why and how we must create partnership relationships with our suppliers. Communication is the essence of that new relationship. As in our own firms, SPC becomes a common ground and a clear, understandable language that we can use in dealing with our suppliers. That's why Quality Age firms require their suppliers to implement SPC.

SPC Facilitates Competition; Makes Rewards and Incentives Meaningful

Various forms of easy-to-devise scorekeeping can be used to measure team performance. But SPC—the great scorekeeper—can help create competition and facilitate rewards and incentives for teams throughout the firm.

That's because SPC measures variation in performance and induces workers to reduce that variation. Reduction in variation equals improvement in quality. Teams of any function can compete with one another simply on the basis of the *rate of improvement* they've achieved in a given period. Or the scores of teams involved in different activities can be put on an equal footing by means of a handicapping system, as used in bowling and golf.

This puts all functions and teams in the firm on a level playing field and can help to ignite a competitive spirit in the work force.

SPC Creates Worker Involvement

Now, there's a magical term for you: *Worker involvement.* Everyone knows that we need worker involvement to improve quality. There's a lot of talk about how to do that. SPC does it.

First of all, the SPC program helps to alleviate an initial impediment to improvement, which is worker skepticism. SPC is real, tangible, something they can see and touch and react to. They see almost at once that this, at last, is not just rhetoric, not just words and exhortations; it's real.

Second, SPC is administered by the workers themselves. They are doing the measuring and the scorekeeping. They are watching the charts, looking for clues, detecting problems, thinking about solutions, implementing them. None of this is being dictated to them by others.

Third, it causes them to take pride in their accomplishments. They can see how they are doing, see how they are improving, see the results of their work. This constant reinforcement brings out the best in the work force.

The essence of SPC's benefits—as well as the essence of the improvement process itself—is communication. It's not a panacea or a magic potion; it takes work, time, and patience. But it creates an environment of communication, wherein the work force learns from the process and works in concert to effect improvement. It causes workers to expect improvement—to expect quality to get better every day.

Training Employees in SPC

Because the workers themselves are going to be at the heart of the SPC program, they'll obviously need some training. But, as with everything else, there's a right way to go about it, and many wrong ways.

I recall the time a major defense contractor on the East Coast decided to implement a full-blown SPC program in one of its plants. It had some 2,000 employees and planned to train them all. I wasn't involved in this program, but I was aware of it and was on good terms with the firm's director of research and development. I asked him if he was taking the SPC training himself.

"Oh," he said, "I sat in for a few minutes, but I took off."

"How come?"

"That stuff they're teaching, it's way over *my* head."

It turned out the line personnel were being trained in things like moment theory, multiple regression, and factor analysis: heavy statistics, in other words—*really* heavy.

I was later told that, after a few days of training, the hourly workers threatened to go out on strike if they had to endure any more. I don't blame them.

Another time, when I was engaged to train a group of plant workers in SPC, their manager was, shall we say, unusually skeptical about their ability to learn.

"Stupid workers," he told me. "They're the stupidest workers I've ever seen. They're lucky if they can find their machines in the morning."

With that endorsement ringing in my ears, I began the class. And it wasn't long before I began to wonder if the manager was right.

I'm a fairly animated instructor, and I was pulling out all the stops, trying to get the students involved, watching them closely to see if I was getting anywhere. It didn't look good. The only feedback I got was blank stares.

At one point I drew three parallel lines on the board—the basic layout of an SPC control chart—and asked the class to tell me which one was the middle line. Only five out of the fifteen got it right.

I knew I had a real problem there. So I halted my lecture and attempted to strike up informal conversations with them, only to find out that they were Hispanics, natives of Mexico, with practically no English.

I went to the manager. "Listen, the reason these people have trouble learning is that most of them don't even speak English."

"So what?"

I stared at him. "It's tough to learn this stuff if you don't understand the language, for Heaven's sake."

He waved a hand. "Don't let 'em fool you. They know more than they're letting on."

Boy, was *he* a big help. I still had to train these people as best I could. Out of desperation I got a Spanish-English dictionary, did some feverish studying, and then resumed the training, using as much Spanish as I could. I had them all charting SPC two days later.

So the first thing to realize about SPC training is this: People don't need degrees in statistics to learn how to use SPC.

And that's a good thing, because the people who need the training the most—line workers, floor workers, hourly workers—often have limited educational backgrounds. What formal education they had may be 10, 15, 20 years in the past. Most of them probably hated being in the classroom for any reason. And the three most hated subjects were probably math, math, and math.

Forcing workers into interminable hours of classroom training is wasteful and counterproductive. Many will spend half the time daydreaming. And, once it's over, most will almost immediately forget 90 percent of what they learned in class, which in turn was probably only about 30 percent of what was taught.

And classroom training is not cheap. In addition to the direct cost of the instructor and materials, there are significant indirect costs in downtime and lost productivity.

So it makes no sense whatsoever to inflict heavy theoretical statistics on these people. They're not equipped to learn it; they feel threatened and resentful at the demand to learn it. Plus, it's unfair. If managers were told they had to endure 80 hours of classroom training in statistics, they'd probably blow their own brains out.

The good news is that students don't need anything like 80 hours of theoretical statistics to become successful at using SPC. You can do a better, more effective, and less costly job in six to twelve hours of classroom training. That's it.

Here, based on my experience over the years, are the elements of a successful SPC training program:

- *Keep classroom sessions short.* At the most, you'll require 18 hours of classroom training. Break it into short sessions of no more than three hours each unless you enjoy the sound of unison snores.

- *Use instructors who speak well.* You'll never get anywhere with professor-types in lab coats who hide behind a podium and drone. The effective trainer is animated, anecdotal, keenly intuitive, and able to relate to the audience. It's someone who projects a sincere desire to help the workers learn.

The instructor must not only understand the subject, but also understand it well enough to make it relevant to the audience, which requires more than just a degree in statistics. Specialized "train the trainers" courses are available for aquiring these skills.

- *Be half instructional, half motivational.* In my view, training is as much a selling job as it is a teaching job. students have to get a feel for the benefits of SPC, how it will help them in the course of their jobs. *Relevancy* is the key here: making SPC relevant to the workers in simple, practical terms. It's also important to introduce and promote the concept of teams and teamwork.

    Further, the instructor must build and maintain rapport with the students and be careful to avoid creating a threatening atmosphere or a classroom environment that embarrasses or humiliates the students.

- *Teach nothing that the people don't need to know and won't use.* Face it: classroom training is only the beginning, the tip of the iceberg. The real training and learning of SPC will take place on the job. So keep theory to a minimum.

    In the classroom, my consultants teach the concept of normal and abnormal variation, the control chart, how to calculate and plot points, and the basics of how to interpret the chart. And every step of the way they relate what they're teaching to the work their students do.

Training Materials

What you teach in the classroom and the manner in which you teach it are important; so is the type of supporting materials you provide to your students. Quality Age firms have found it very effective to provide students with some form of simple, easy-to-use workbook.

Keep in mind that your students come from different backgrounds and have different educational levels. Learning rates vary substantially. A textbook or workbook of some sort not only serves to reinforce the classroom learning, it also enables students to study and to learn at their own pace.

But avoid heavy scholarly treatises. The book should be relatively simple, relatively pertinent, and relatively entertaining. Otherwise, the students won't use it, so what's the point?

Another reason to provide a textbook or workbook to the students is its positive psychological impact. I once surveyed a group of workers after implementing SPC in their operation; when asked what they felt was the best element of the process, they overwhelmingly cited the training workbooks. They felt that management was at last getting serious about an improvement program—serious enough to provide workers with textbooks they could use and keep. It meant a lot to them.

Implementation: Where the Real Training Begins

Many firms believe that the training process is complete when the classes are over. On the contrary: when the classes are over and the people return to work, the training has only begun.

Implementing SPC on the job is the real challenge. In successful SPC, training is only about 10 percent of the equation; implementation is the other 90 percent. Put another way, you can have a successful SPC program with mediocre training if you put enough effort into implementation; the training can be first-rate but the SPC program will die on the vine if implementation isn't there.

The key to this—and I can't overstate its importance—is to *start using SPC on the job the instant training is over.* I've seen firms invest incredible amounts of money, time, and other resources on the design and the training aspects of their SPC program only to have everything go down the chute because they waited a week or even a month after training to start using it in the operation.

I believe in taking students directly from the classroom to their workstations and starting to use SPC there immediately. If the instruction has been done correctly, students are motivated at this point. Their learning is fresh in their minds. They're intrigued about SPC and want to see it in action. Strike while the iron is hot!

Another reason to start using SPC immediately is that classroom training tends to emphasize the "nuts and bolts" of SPC and only vaguely gets into the most critical aspect: interpreting the charts.

Chart interpretation is no more difficult than looking at a picture and observing patterns. But the critical factor is that interpretation is very specific to the particular operation being charted. There's more to it than memorizing a couple of rules. Interpreting charts requires a new attitude, a questioning, inquisitive attitude, a whole new way of thinking.

There's really no way to teach that in the classroom; you can only do that in real life. And it takes time to learn—months, usually. But it's worth it. With coaching, workers will learn to read the signals that the charts are sending. They'll learn how to tell the likely causes of problems. Again, I must emphasize that knowledge of statistics is not vital to this—but knowledge of the process is. And who's more knowledgeable about the process than the people who work in it every day?

With training, time, patience, and help, everyone will learn how SPC can help them. They'll see things getting better. They'll achieve individual and group successes. And once this happens, the program will develop a life of its own.

Other Training Issues

In real life, training never stops. You inevitably have turnover, with new personnel coming into the picture, requiring training. And it's often helpful to provide refresher training to past students.

For these reasons, it's helpful to have on hand SPC training programs on videotape. It's well worth the investment, as opposed to hiring someone from the outside to come in repeatedly.

I also think it's important that all training programs and materials be consistent throughout your organization, whether your firm consists of two departments in one building or 500 subsidiaries worldwide.

Scorekeeping in general, and SPC in particular, are at the heart of Integrated Quality Management. They're central to the entire improvement effort. Statistical Process Control is at the heart of most Japanese firms. It underpins the dramatic turnaround of Ford Motor Company. It's a tool that is now mandated by firms such as IBM, General Electric, Peterbilt, Hewlett-Packard, General Dynamics and most of the Fortune 500.

7

Advanced Tools

Several years ago, I was engaged to design and implement an improvement program for a huge West Coast distribution firm. Following my normal routine, I started out simply by walking around, observing, making notes, interviewing people. It was clear from the outset that they really needed help.

I started out in the area called Delivery. There, orders were put together and products were pulled from inventory and sent out to their destinations. I walked around with the foreman, looking things over, watching the activity closely. And there seemed to be lots of activity: people milling around everywhere. But when you looked closely, there didn't seem to be a lot of work really getting done. And the foreman confirmed this.

"We're just not getting *anything* done here," he complained. "We're always behind, always struggling, always late. What it comes down to is, none of these people is really putting any effort into the job."

I'd been watching the activity for several minutes, and one worker in particular caught my eye. Unlike the others, he was really working hard—an absolute dynamo, always on the go, practically killing himself.

I said to the foreman, "How about that guy? He seems to be working pretty hard."

"Jim? Oh, yeah," the foreman sighed. "I wish my workers were all like that. But we're going to lose him."

"How come?"

"He won't pass his 90-day review."

I was puzzled. "How come? He's doing the work of the next 10 guys put together."

"I know, but he makes too many errors. His error rate is going to kill him. Bad quality, real bad quality."

"Well," I conceded, "quality's important, but . . ."

"Quality is everything," the foreman said. "At least around here it is."

"I don't understand."

"Let me explain, then. Around here, our people are rated only on quality. Only by the number of errors they make. The fewer the errors, the higher their rating. That means that guys like Jim over there, who put out tons of work, almost never last very long. And even if they do, they never win any awards or anything. When you do as much work as they do, you're bound to commit more errors than people who do less work. Get it?"

"I guess so." I was so floored by this, I hardly knew what to say. "Let me ask you this. Who usually wins the awards? Anybody in particular?"

"That would be Dave. Dave usually wins, hands down."

I looked around at the workers. "Which one is he? I don't see him here."

"Oh, he's hardly ever around. That's how come he usually wins." The foreman lowered his voice. "He hardly ever does any work, see? When the raters come around, they track him down and ask him to do some work so they have samples to rate him on. So he does a job or two, does them perfectly, zero errors, *bing!* He wins."

I thought for a minute, then looked the foreman in the eye. "Tell me. Does this really strike you as a good incentive system?"

He shrugged. "No. It's the pits. But that's how we're told to handle it. It comes straight from topside. We rate 'em on quality and only quality. Period."

"Well," I observed, "if you want productivity, that's got to figure into the incentive system somewhere, don't you think?"

"I'm not sure the incentive program's really important, anyway," he answered. "People aren't money-motivated."

"They aren't?"

"No."

"How about you?" I pressed. "Don't *you* want to make more money?"

"Sure I do."

"Then how can you say people aren't . . ."

"I'm the exception."

This illustrates one of the Quality Age pitfalls: the tendency to push for quality to the exclusion of everything else—even to the extent of creating incentive programs that emphasize quality only. Inevitably, these produce the negative results I witnessed at the distribution firm.

We need just as much emphasis on productivity. As we discussed in Chapter 2, productivity contributes to customer satisfaction because it enables us to produce our products or services at prices our customers are willing to pay.

Productivity is, in fact, a subset of quality; yet quality and productivity remain opposing forces in many stagnant firms. They are often seperate entities consisting of seperate groups of employees with seperate and conflicting imperatives.

"Quality" people don't care about how much work is done; they only care about meeting specifications and minimizing defects. "Productivity" people care about that output number, how much gets done. They resist the efforts of "quality" people just as "quality" people are always pushing to slow things up and do them better.

Incentive programs emphasizing quality at the expense of productivity, or vice versa, tend to make things worse, not better. Because of that, many quality gurus have advocated eliminating productivity incentive programs altogether. But eliminaiting incentives deprives us of one of the best motivation devices ever invented. So efforts have been made to create a performance score uniting quality and productivity.

Usually, these efforts employ some form of what I call the *subtraction method*. To get the score, you take the total number produced and subtract the number of defective items. One big flaw in this approach is that workers realize that they can circumvent the intent by jacking production up to the skies. That will make the combined index look good, but it does little to cause employees to focus on quality and productivity at the same time.

Such an approach has additional pitfalls:

- It does not take into account the *material costs* of the defective product that is produced.

- It does not take into account the *labor cost* of the defective product—which is, in fact, labor costs from the entire process stream.

- It does not take into account the production of *marginal products* that may pass inspection, yet not work as well in the field, mate as well with other products, or wear as long.

- It does not take into account the *bad products* that are always missed by inspection.

- It does nothing to advance our efforts toward *constant improvement*. Rather, workers strive only to achieve the minimum acceptable quality level and produce as fast as humanly possible.

The subtraction method does not in fact unite quality and productivity scorekeeping into a common index. It does not resolve the perceived conflict between the two. Nor does it eliminate the rivalry that hampers constant improvement and produces stagnation.

The Quality/Productivity Index

There is, however, a way to produce a common index of performance. It's one that I created for the distribution firm we talked about, as well as for other firms. I call it the *quality/productivity index* (QPI), and it is in fact a true index of performance.

The key to creating an effective QPI is deciding how to measure *quality* realistically. You have to identify the true quality issues and weight them. Some things are more important than others. When you're making aircraft engines, for example, a defect in the wiring harness is clearly an error, a quality problem—a life-and-death issue, actually. We'd call that a defect.

We may also call a scratch on the exhaust manifold a defect. But is it a defect in the same sense that a flaw in the wiring harness is a defect? Certainly not. In short, we have to define in precise terms what a *defect* is. Then we have to rank those defects, prioritize them. Defects that rank high on the list must affect our performance score more seriously than defects that rank lower.

This exercise in definition can be a real education for management and workers alike. It helps clear away the clutter and focus on what's really important.

In practice, the occurrence of defects is then turned into a quality factor that is *multiplied* against productivity. The result is the quality/productivity index.

Because it is a function of multiplication, QPI gives a much more realistic picture of true performance. It builds in an estimate of the impact of the "hidden" and "unknown" factors such as material and labor cost, undetected problems, marginal products.

This form of QPI is, admittedly, very simplistic. It's an ideal starting point, though, and a good way to get the work force accustomed to working with a common index of performance. After it's been in place for a while, you'd do well to employ the services of a professional firm to help you identify more precise forms of measurement and evaluation.

QPI works, for many of the same reasons that the other scientific scorekeeping methods, such as SPC, work:

- It puts the forces of quality and productivity on the same side. People focus not on one or the other anymore, but on both together. Their best interest becomes the same as the firm's best interest: to produce the largest possible number of quality products and services.

- The QPI creates another arena for incentives and rewards. This reinforces the concept of teams and self-competition. Teams can compete with themselves or with one another based on the rate of improvement in the QPI, to cite just one example.

- The QPI is a tool that facilitates communication. Production people become aware of the quality issues; quality people now have a reason to want production to succeed. The two elements now work together to effect improvement in both areas—because it's in their interest to do so.

- The QPI provides a form of historical record: like SPC, it tells us what's going on with the process. We can track the QPI over time, see how much we've improved, and see how changes affect it.

The QPI is just another example of how *scientific scorekeeping* produces and perpetuates constant improvement.

Design of Experiments (DOE)

I'll never forget a golf outing I went on about five years ago. I'm a pretty decent golfer—not the world's greatest, but I usually hold my own. Not this time, though. My driving had just plain fallen apart. I tried to settle down and get my act together. I tried everything I could think of to get back on track, and nothing helped. Everything, in fact, just made my driving worse.

The other members of our foursome knew my game pretty well and saw that I was having trouble. Since this was a friendly game, they were willing, even eager, to offer me all kinds of free advice.

One guy said I was using the wrong kind of clubs. "Clubs with stiff shafts are better," he told me.

Another was something of an expert on tees. "You're setting your tee height too high," he said. "You're getting under the ball too much. Set your tee height lower."

The third player had been watching me in profile, evidently doing all kinds of arithmetic in his head. "The problem is your backswing," he announced. "It's too flat. You need to arc it more."

Being anxious to do well, I took all this advice to heart. And it occurred to me that there were a lot of other factors to consider. Some people believe that the type of ball you use makes a difference. The type of stance is thought to be important, too: open or closed. There are several types of grip; different kinds of shoes; one glove, two gloves, no gloves at all . . .

There were, in fact, dozens of factors to consider: dozens of factors and literally hundreds of combinations of them. How could I find the best possible combination of all those factors?

One way would be to try every single combination. I could play a round of golf using each combination, keep track of the scores, analyze them at the end, and pick out the one that worked the best. Now, I love golf, but I don't want to invest the five years of my life that it would probably take to do this!

There has to be a way to sort through all this clutter to find the best possible combination without spending the rest of our lives doing it.

In our businesses, we face the same sort of situation every day: all kinds of variables, factors, possible combinations. Nothing is ever absolute to begin with, and everything changes constantly.

- When we're making something, whether it's a part for an engine, a deluxe pizza to go, a chemical mixture, a television set, or a pair of sneakers, there is a myriad of possible factors—various types of raw material and ingredients and multiple suppliers for all; methods and procedures; equipment; labor; speed; and more.

- The marketplace is an assemblage of wheels within wheels within wheels—different countries and cultures, composed of different demographic segments, made up of unique individuals whose needs, expectations and perceptions are in a constant state of flux.

- Even in the administration of our firms, there are multiple options at each step—constant choices to be made, innumerable combinations. To cite just one example, we may think our paperwork flow is as efficient as is humanly possible, but odds are it isn't. There's always room to improve. The question is, where do we start?

Experimentation is an obvious way to find the best possible combination. But how do we proceed? Do I experiment with every possible combination of factors—and invest five years of my life in the process—to find the best possible combination of all the factors affecting my golf swing?

In our firms, do we experiment with every possible combination to find the best one? Obviously not. If we did, we'd find ourselves becoming professional experimenters with no time left over to do our real work. There's not much future in that.

But this doesn't mean that we can't find the best possible combination. All we have to do is bring a little science to the experimentation process. We need a tool that helps us look efficiently at the effect of the various combinations at one time—a tool that greatly reduces the number of experiments we must run and, correspondingly, the amount of time, labor, and other resources we must invest. But this tool must, nevertheless, give us scientifically proven and predictable results.

Just such a tool is in constant use by Quality Age firms like Ford Motor, IBM, and Dupont. It is an experimental method called *design of experiments* (DOE). DOE is a scientific way of structuring, conducting, and evaluating experiments to show very clearly which factors are important and which combination of factors gives us the result we want—without the need for multiple tests of all possible factors.

But there's a key difference between SPC and DOE. SPC gives us a picture of the process *as it is* and helps us detect the intrusion of variation due to assignable causes. DOE is a statistical tool that takes us a step forward. It allows us to ask "what if"; it helps us answer questions, deal with changes, and make refinements in the most efficient and cost-effective way.

Ford's top managers have become such believers in DOE that they not only use it throughout the organization, they are also beginning to require their suppliers to learn and use it, just as they do with SPC. They do this because they've proven to themselves that DOE is a low-cost, low-investment way to effect higher quality.

What about skill levels, training, and the cost to get into DOE? It's a bit more advanced than SPC, but even so DOE is not beyond the reach of the average worker. Ford has begun training its floor personnel in selected areas in the concept and application of DOE.

All it really takes is some basic training in the method, using the same criteria as SPC; there are seminars and workbooks available that provide the basics. Then, as with SPC, you learn by doing. It's also important to know that inexpensive computer software is widely available to handle virtually all the number-crunching for you.

Scorekeeping: Simple and Safe When Used As Directed

Statistical scorekeeping tools such as SPC, QPI and DOE can be used with great effect in virtually any kind of operation. Whether you operate a fast food facility, manufacture nuts and bolts, provide brokerage or financial services, run a warehouse or a delivery service or a sales firm, scorekeeping helps make quality enduring and improvement permanent. It also shows us where we stand, and encourages us to ask ourselves; "Have we improved?"

At this point, you may be wondering, "If that's so, and if SPC and DOE and the other tools are so great, why doesn't everybody use them?"

I think there are a couple of reasons. First, many firms simply don't understand the techniques or have the mistaken notion that they are not applicable to their particular environment. One goal of this book is to correct those notions by demystifying the techniques, putting them into practical perspective, and illustrating by example.

Second, and even more pervasive, is the idea that statistical scorekeeping methods are "above our heads." Fear, plain and simple, has caused many of us to shun these proven methods. And that is tragic—because there's no need to be afraid or intimidated.

Much of the fear, it seems to me, comes from the jargon that is employed in these methods. People hear terms like "sigma," "grand mean," "signal to noise," and others—and run for cover. This is unfortunate. The terms are easy to understand

and use once you've had a little bit of simple training and on-the-job experience. And jargon itself is a fact of life in our businesses, anyway.

Once, a government man said to me, "When we look at the UMR, we see from the MISSER files that the DMOs were going to go with the RDs. I'll take it up with the CO and the XO." It sounded like gibberish—till I learned what the terms meant.

The same thing is true with statistical methods. There's nothing scary about them at all. In Japan, statistical scorekeeping methods are, literally, second nature. Nobody questions their usefulness. The Japanese embraced tools *that we Americans invented in the first place,* refined them, perfected them, and are now clubbing us over the head with them—while many American firms waste precious time hanging back, fearing the unknown, debating the unquestionable, and trying to play "catch-up."

8

Integrated Quality Management: Step by Step

When you start a new business, you begin hungry. You grab all the work that comes along simply to survive. You also begin, in most cases, in a state of ignorance. You're learning far more from your customers than they're learning from you. You have to learn at a dizzying pace just to get off the ground.

That was my situation back in the early days of my quality/productivity consulting practice. My main service back then was SPC training and implementation. And I was hungry, all right. I took any work I could get.

One very early client was a certain fastener firm that was experiencing the garden variety of quality and productivity problems. It was losing business fast and its managers knew that something had to be done. They'd become enamored of the concept of SPC and hired me to train their workers.

Well, I gave it my best shot. I went out there and conducted SPC training classes for their people. Although all seemed to go well, I came back home with a niggling feeling of doubt. I'd done what I'd been hired to do, and I believed that I had done it well. But I had a feeling that something was missing.

A couple of months later, the firm's president called me. He wanted to meet with me right away. He sounded very anxious and very unhappy. Of course, I've always had a policy of absolute satisfaction, and if there was a problem with the work I'd done, I intended to do whatever I had to do to fix it. So I went out to see him.

When we met in his office, I asked, "So, was there some problem with the SPC training?"

"No, not at all," the president said. "Everybody raved over how good the training and the presentation were. They were fired up like you wouldn't believe. "

"But there's a problem?"

"Sure is."

"Are the people doing the SPC charting?"

"Oh, absolutely." He gestured at a pile of paper on his desk. "We've got charts coming out our ears. That's not the problem."

"Then what is it?"

He stared at me. "We've still got defects."

"Well, I . . ."

"Defects!" he repeated. "We're still making bad products! I just don't understand it. We spent all that money on the training, we're doing all the charting we're supposed to, and we've still got defects. I can't figure out why that is."

As I said, in your early days the learning curve is very steep. And that experience taught me three lessons: one vital and immediate, the others a bit more subtle but, in the long run, even more important.

The first lesson was: *You can't expect immediate gratification.* Early victories, yes. Promising signs, certainly. But overnight perfection? No way. No matter how much you spend, how hard you work, or how much pressure you apply, the most sophisticated and well-thought-out program in the world isn't going to transform your firm into a Quality Age company overnight.

The president of the fastener firm, 90 days into the program, was unhappy with its lack of results. First of all, it was clearly too early to expect a dramatic turnaround. Second, he hadn't been taught to seek out the small victories that were undoubtedly all around him.

The second lesson is even more far-reaching. *No single tool or program can do the job alone—not even SPC.* I call SPC "the great scorekeeper," and I truly believe that no single tool is as effective in addressing all the aspects of continuous improvement. SPC, by itself, can make things better. But it can't do the job alone, no matter how effectively it's used.

SPC training in a vacuum is like a professional basketball team with one superstar player and four mediocre ones. The superstar sets scoring records galore, makes the All-Star team every year, gets his picture in the papers. But his team? His team always finishes well back in the pack.

The fastener firm had hired me for SPC training, and only SPC training. We still get assignments like that, and our consultants carry them out as best they can. But I never stop stressing the important message wherever I go: SPC, for all its benefits, is only part of the story.

The third lesson is just as difficult to get across to new clients: *Training is but 10 percent of the equation; the other 90 percent is implementation.* How you *use* what you learn, in other words, is more important than how *well* you learn it.

I've seen firms go out and get really terrible training: boring, excessively complex, theoretical, inappropriate, and hideously expensive. Yet they've gone on to transform themselves successfully into Quality Age firms. Why? Because they overcame the deficiencies of their training with an overall plan that was well-thought-out and vigorously pursued.

On the other hand, I've seen some of the finest training ever developed go down the chute because it was followed up with—well—nothing. The training we furnished to the fastener firm was, by all accounts, excellent. I did what I was hired to do and went home when I was done. They expected the training to do the trick and had no plan for putting the training to work.

The fastener firm experience led me to modify the approach my consultants and I take with all our clients.

- We stress that there are no quick fixes. Improvement is a long-term process, requiring persistence if it is to succeed.
- We don't rely on SPC alone. We've united all the tools: SPC, quality function deployment, design of experiments, and problem solving.

These factors, taken together with the quality image and the unification of quality and productivity, constitute Integrated Quality Management—a proven quality improvement program based on *scorekeeping* and *communication*.

- I've coordinated all these factors into an implementation plan that works. I call that plan Integrated Quality Management because it unites all the essential elements of my program. Its basic foundation is *scorekeeping* and *communication*.

In the previous seven chapters, we've dealt with all these issues in some detail. Those seven chapters function, in a sense, as a form of training and orientation. But, as I said, training and orientation are only the beginning; *implementation* is the key to success. Successful implementation is what makes improvement continuous, autonomous, and self-sustaining.

The purpose of this chapter is to spell out, in step-by-step fashion, the process of implementing Integrated Quality Management. Here, I'll put all the philosophies and tools into context, raising a few new issues, reviewing the rest, and showing how they work together.

Where Do We Start?

The improvement process is, at best, difficult. We would like to implement it universally; ultimately, that is our goal. But, practically speaking, it's virtually impossible to do that all at once in very large firms with many sites, processes, and functions.

Some of the steps—such as obtaining management commitment, establishing the quality image department or team, creating partnership relationships with suppliers, identifying the customer goal, and translating it into the process through quality function deployment—are "topside" activities that must be carried out, regardless of the size of the operation.

But, with regard to the other steps, I recommend what I call a *modular approach* to implementation. We select one process or activity with which to begin. We use that experience and the successes it obtains to "feed" the process of implementation with other process modules.

The sequence of modular implementation has to be thought through in advance. Where do we start?

- I recommend selecting a module for which the supplied product is found to be relatively consistent and trouble-free. This allows you to concentrate on internal improvement.

- Start with a process that is relatively small and self-contained—one that you feel has the greatest likelihood of success. This is a judgment call.

- Start with a process that is not under a lot of pressure for productivity and is not operating at peak capacity.

Early on, you can decide with which module to start. You may revise that decision after conducting the survey and analysis in Step 3, discussed later.

Step 1: Develop a Written Plan

The implementation process is always governed by a written plan, and before doing anything else you must sketch out the first one. The plan tentatively specifies the initial (pilot) module, the expected results, and a timetable of implementation steps. The plan also includes a general idea of scheduling implementation for other modules.

The plan is very important because without it you're flying blind. It's not enough to say, "Well, we're going to do some training, and then we're going to do some charting, and we'll have some team meetings and stuff." With that approach, things eventually grind to a halt. You stop generating results, and the program dies.

But you obviously can't engrave the plan in stone at this point. You'll constantly be revising and updating it as the process of implementation moves forward.

Step 2: Ensure Top
Management Commitment

In Chapter 4, we discussed at length the necessity for top management commitment. Without it, the succeeding implementation steps will never happen; without it, you might as well forget the whole thing.

Step 3: Conduct a Survey and Analysis

The next step is to perform an exhaustive study of the firm and its processes. I need to stress here that this is not a search for guilty parties or an attempt to diagnose problems. It is simply a detailed study of how things stand with the process. A typical survey and analysis includes the following:

- A detailed diagram of the process stream, detailing what each step receives, what it does, and what it delivers.
- A summary of major problems perceived with the process.
- Identification of the critical process points. These are the places where we'll eventually do our SPC charting, based on the guidelines suggested in Chapter 6.
- An assessment of the workers: education and skill levels and attitudes toward the firm, the product, and the customers.

That last step is particularly important because, ultimately, what the workers do determines the success or the failure of the program.

In fact, the process of conducting the survey and analysis can function as an initial selling effort for the program. Tour the process, talk to the workers, and really get down to cases with them. Find out how *they* feel, what *they* believe the problems really are. Don't talk about scorekeeping, SPC, or anything else yet; just get them to talk and listen.

They have a wealth of knowledge and experience that I guarantee they'll share with you if you are receptive. They'll share it because they'll feel flattered to be asked after having had their opinions bottled up for so long.

Assessing worker skill levels will also give you a feel as to the level of training you'll need to conduct later. You may find, as General Motors did, that it's necessary to conduct a two-hour class on how to use a four-function calculator. It's better to know that sort of thing early so you can deal with it.

After you've evaluated the survey and analysis, go back to the plan and make any needed changes in steps and timing. You may also change your mind about which module to implement first.

One final word about the survey and analysis: consider engaging an outside expert to perform this step for you. An outside expert brings a wealth of experience to the task. Further—and more critical—an outsider will not hesitate to be direct and blunt with top management. Conversely, middle management will tend to be more honest with an outsider. He or she does not have to worry about company politics, as does even the most earnest and dedicated insider.

Step 4: Create a Quality Image Team or Department

In Chapter 1 we talked about that notoriously unacknowledged aspect of quality: your firm's quality image, the *perception* the outside world has of your firm and its quality. I recommend establishing a separate and dedicated team or department, charged with monitoring quality image. Its general responsibilities should be to

- Survey current and former customers and scientifically selected samples of prospects to determine specifically what the firm's quality image is.

- Survey employees to determine what they think the firm's quality image is and should be.

- Assess each of the firm's departments (the receptionists bookkeeping, clerical, accounting, traffic, warehousing,

- etc.) to assess its impact, positive or negative, on the quality image. It's vital that this assessment include the sales department, whose activities have a major impact on customer perception and expectation.

- Evaluate the firm's public communications (advertising, public relations, etc.) to assess what quality image these activities are projecting.

- Develop ways to improve the quality image; recommend detailed plans to management.

- With scientific surveying, scorekeeping, and analysis, monitor the quality image on an ongoing basis.

Step 5: Identify and Monitor the Customer Goal

In the final analysis, quality is, as I discussed in Chapter 1, a unique relationship between customer's *expectation* and the customer's *perception of value received*. We can express this relationship as a formula:

$$\text{Quality} = \frac{\text{Customer perception of value received}}{\text{Customer expectation}}$$

I call this relationship the *customer goal,* and it varies from firm to firm, product to product, time to time. It is in a constant state of evolution. The extent to which you meet this customer goal governs your ability to generate new business, repeat business, growth, and market share.

- What are the five things you like about our product or service today?

- What are the five things you dislike about our product or service today?

- What is it that has made you do business with us?

- What is it that has prevented you from doing business with us?

- What must we do to ensure that you will do business with us again?

Once again, don't overlook the wealth of knowledge and experience that resides in your work force: not just people with public contact responsibilities, but *everyone*. Ask these same questions of them. Evaluate the responses; from these, you will be able to assemble a detailed, cogent customer goal.

As I've pointed out, this is not a one-time exercise. The forces of change are always at work. Maintain continuous contact with customers and prospects—directly, and through internal channels. Look for trends in the customer goal; most especially, keep an eye on the horizon and develop an ability to *anticipate* what the customer goal will look like down the road. That, along with the ability to react quickly, is the key to strengthening your competitive position.

Step 6: Develop Partnership Relationships with Suppliers

In Chapter 3 we discussed how today's Quality Age firms have made major improvements in their own quality and productivity by completely transforming their relationships with their suppliers. We can no longer base supplier relationships strictly on price charged by the supplier. Such an approach causes us to do business with multiple suppliers for each acquired product or service, which is very costly to us in several different ways.

Irrespective of how quickly you implement Integrated Quality Management within your own firm, the effort to overhaul supplier relationships must begin early—right after you obtain management commitment to the plan. That's because it can take a lot of time to accomplish. The faster you've developed new supplier relationships, the faster you'll see overall improvement in your own process, products, and services.

As I've said, the philosophy behind this effort, as practiced by many Quality Age firms, is, "What's good for us must be good for our suppliers." Pursue this step in a positive, not a negative, way. Here again are the basic steps required to establish partnership relationships with your suppliers:

- *Recognize that suppliers are part of your company—not outsiders.*

- *Involve your purchasers in the improvement effort from the beginning.* They must be involved in every step: identifying the customer goal, translating that goal back into the process, training, and implementing scorekeeping methods. All this involvement is aimed at keeping purchasers aware of the impact that the supplied products and services have on the internal process.

- *Recognize that the cost of aquired product includes more than the price charged.* It includes processing cost, warranty expense, cost of impact on the quality image, and cost of lost business.

- *Advise suppliers of your new improvement effort at the very beginning.* Advise them that they'll be seeing significant changes in the way you do business. Offer them your assistance with improvement programs of their own.

- *Begin to negotiate long-term sole-source contracts with selected suppliers to reduce the size of your supplier network.* These contracts must include the suppliers' commitment to implement an improvement program of their own; an agreement on reporting requirements; gradual price concessions; indemnification; and sharing of research and development activities.

- *Monitor adherence to supplier agreements vigorously.* Study your suppliers' reports on the progress of their own improvement efforts. Audit their facilities yourself if necessary.

Step 7: Translate the Customer Goal into Your Process (Quality Function Deployment)

As discussed in Chapter 2, it's important to determine in specific detail exactly what your customers expect in your product or service. Once you've done this (and I stress that it's an ongoing effort), you may find that what your customers want differs in many respects from what you've actually been offering to them. You will therefore have to make changes in your process; reorient it so that what it is producing is consistent with the customer goal.

This reorientation process does not start at the design phase of our process. That's been a traditional problem among stagnant firms: the tendency to begin with the design phase instead of beginning with the customer goal. Too often people "design it, then try to sell it." Customer goal translation is really a communications vehicle. You take what the customer is communicating to you and translate that back into the process, step by step, all the way back to the beginning.

The forum for this is a kind of brainstorming session, a team meeting consisting of representatives from every step in the process, from sales, marketing, and distribution all the way back to design and R&D.

The steps outlined in Chapter 2 establish a solid foundation for Integrated Quality Management. Now you're ready to put all this planning into action.

Step 8: Choose Appropriate Staff

As part of its incredible turnaround, Ford Motor Company has been putting sustained emphasis on reducing its supplier network and establishing partnership relationships with its suppliers. One aspect of this approach has been the requirement that Ford suppliers implement SPC within their organizations.

Some firms—and this is not limited to Ford suppliers—have a fundamental misconception about how SPC is implemented. Here's an example, related to me by a Ford executive.

The president of a supplier firm met with a Ford purchasing agent after making a study of SPC. "Listen, Charlie," the president said, "I've looked over this SPC thing, and I have to agree with you; it's a great tool and it'll do a lot for us."

"I'm glad to hear it," the Ford man said. "It's certainly working for us."

"Yeah, I know. But here's the thing, Charlie; there are some costs attendant to putting SPC in, and I've figured them all up, and I wanted to go over them with you. Pretty heavy."

"Heavy?" the Ford man echoed. "Sure, there's some cost, but . . . "

"Here's what I've got," the supplier said briskly. "I did this analysis, and what I've figured out is the incremental cost of putting SPC in. This is the whole shooting match, top to bottom. The incremental cost the first year is going to be $10,716,000."

The Ford man stared. "Ten mil? You've got to be kidding."

"Heck no, I'm not joking. Now here's my idea . . ."

"Ten million bucks," the Ford man mused.

"You guys want me to do it, right? I wouldn't be doing it except you're a major customer and you're requiring me to do it . . ."

"Ten million; that just doesn't make sense," the Ford man said.

". . . and I *want* to do it, you understand, but I can't handle that big an expense . . ."

"There's just no way it's 10 million," the Ford man said.

". . . and I don't expect you guys to pay it, either. That's not what I'm proposing at all," the supplier churned on. "What I figure is fair is, you guys pay half. I'll absorb the other half."

"Hold it," the Ford man said. "Let's go over your analysis. There's something wrong."

"Sure, Charlie."

The supplier handed the analysis over. The Ford man skimmed through it, then stopped and stared. "Charters?" he whispered.

"Yeah," the supplier said earnestly. "This SPC thing; you do charting, right? So I'm going to need to hire charters. I figure we need to hire 60 or 70 of them. Maybe more later."

The Ford man, needless to say, made haste to rectify this common misconception. SPC charting must be done by the first line employees themselves. After all, its sole purpose is to get the people doing the work more involved in finding and correcting problems. You want to motivate them to ask questions constantly, to pay attention to what's going on. To add yet another peripheral organization to do that would be a total waste.

One frequent objection to the whole SPC concept is, "Our people are too busy now. They're not getting enough done as it is. If we make them do all this charting, they'll get even less done." In practice, the time requirements for doing SPC charting are minimal, and the benefits in terms of quality and productivity more than make up for them.

So there's no need to hire charters as part of your improvement program. But it is necessary to do a minimal amount of additional staffing. This need not be incremental, but it's important to create positions dedicated to monitoring the SPC program.

The number of positions you create depends on the size of your firm. In most situations, you'll need to create an SPC manager position to report to top management, supervising the work of SPC coordinators. I've found that the average SPC coordinator can adequately supervise the SPC activities of 100 to 400 personnel.

What are the prerequisites for a successful SPC coordinator?

- The SPC coordinator or manager need *not* be a statistician to be effective. It is important that the person have some math background and be fairly comfortable with it. I've found that people with some graduate training in one of the sciences that utilizes statistics—such as experimental psychology—often have as good an educational background than people who have degrees in theoretical statistics.

- It's vital that the SPC coordinator be comfortable dealing with all sorts of people in all sorts of situations. The coordinator must be able to talk to hourly workers as effectively as with top management. In other words, the job requires strong people skills.

The person selected to be SPC coordinator or SPC manager should undergo SPC training before the rest of the work force.

Most especially, SPC coordinators should take advanced training in SPC chart interpretation, which will be one of their principal functions.

SPC coordinators and managers should be involved in the survey and analysis as well as in the other key IQM activities. It's important, too, that these individuals be properly placed in the political hierarchy; SPC coordinators and managers should report to a member of top management. In general, we want this person to have authority over both quality and productivity, to ensure that one is not favored to the exclusion of the other.

I've said that candidates for SPC coordinators and managers need not be degreed statisticians. By that, I don't mean to suggest that you shouldn't have a professional statistician on staff somewhere. The services of a theoretical statistician can be very helpful in the interpretation of complex SPC chart situations, as well as in the development and analysis of advanced scorekeeping techniques (such as the quality/productivity index) and in the design and evaluation of experiments.

Step 9: Train the Work Force

Now you're ready to train the work force in the fundamental scorekeeping technique: Statistical Process Control (SPC).

We talked about the dos and don'ts of training in Chapter 6. The key points to remember about effective training are:

- *Teach personnel only what they need to know; avoid complex and intimidating theories.*
- *Effective training is 50 percent motivational and 50 percent instructional.*
- *Keep training brief, to the point, and as entertaining as possible.*
- *Provide simple training aids that workers can use and keep.*
- *Go from the training environment to the work environment immediately.*
- *Develop on-staff expertise in chart interpretation.*

Step 10: Commence Team Activities

A team should be established for each process function. Another team should be assembled in which each function is represented. Team meetings should be held regularly; the meetings themselves should be short, to the point, and governed by an agenda. Discussion of scorekeeping results should be at the heart of the agenda. Teams should also evaluate problems that have arisen as well as possible solutions.

Other team activities include

- *Publicizing victories and success stories.* As the program gets under way, it's absolutely vital that every success, no matter how small, be publicized. This has an extremely powerful reinforcing effect.

- *Establishing positive competition.* Individual teams can compete with themselves—current results versus past results. Teams can also compete with one another. An excellent basis for team competition is rate of improvement, as indicated by SPC scorekeeping. The incentives and rewards for success need not be monetary; they can include things like paid days off, company-sponsored parties, plaques, and the like. The possibilities here are endless, but it's vital that the victories themselves, and the rewards earned, be publicized.

- *Systematic problem solving.* This is a disciplined technique for identifying, isolating, and solving business problems. Mastery of the technique requires specialized training and (like everything else) practice, but it is, in my experience, well worhtwhile. Some firms create ad hoc problem-solving teams; I believe that problem solving is a tool that every process team should have in its arsenal.

Step 11: Begin Development and Use of Advanced Scorekeeping Techniques

SPC is an incredibly powerful tool, and it can take as long as a year to implement it and realize its ongoing benefits fully.

Though implementing SPC will be your pre-eminent effort in the early days, I also recommend that you start equipping yourself with the advanced scorekeeping tools that we've discussed:

- *The quality/productivity index.* The QPI is a common index that takes into account both quality and productivity. When you keep score this way, the rivalry between the two efforts disappears.
- *Design of experiments.* DOE is a scientific method of testing the combinations of options in a relatively simple and inexpensive way. It helps you find the best possible combination without having to "keep guessing till you get it right."

There it is, in 11 general steps: Integrated Quality Management in sequence. But once you're under way, how will you know that it's working? Here are some guidelines.

Energy and Dynamism among Your People

One of the most startling changes in a firm making the transformation is that the very *atmosphere* becomes electric with vitality. It's not something that's immediately measurable; it's something that you can feel. But there are also several concrete ways to measure the rising level of dynamism:

- *Drastic rise in employee suggestions.* Once employees realize that their input is welcome, is encouraged, and (most important) makes a difference, the suggestions simply start to pour in. I don't suggest for a minute that every single suggestion is going to change the world, but there will be plenty of nuggets.
- *Steady stream of success stories.* If the volume of these ever starts to taper off, watch out! It won't necessarily mean that there aren't as many any more; what it will mean is that people are getting slack about publicizing them.

- *Decreased turnover*. People who are involved in their work, committed to it, successful at it, and having fun at it are much less likely to want to change jobs.
- *Improved survey results*. It's useful to poll employees periodically on their feelings and attitudes toward the firm and their jobs. In a dynamic environment, these survey scores will show steady improvement.

Reduction in "Doing It Over"

Typical of the stagnant firm is the syndrome of "doing it over." It becomes so pervasive that no one ever questions it. The most obvious form of "doing it over" is replacing defective products or repeating incorrectly performed services. A less obvious form—but a costlier one—is the repeated *redesign* of a new product or service. This results from the isolation of the design phase from the rest of the process and from the expectations of the customer.

When Integrated Quality Management gets under way, you will observe a constant and ongoing reduction of both types of "doing it over." By keeping score on variation, identifying its causes, and eliminating them, you'll begin to achieve the sought-after goal of "doing it right the first time." There'll be less scrap, less rework, less "doing it over," and less expense, too.

By designing products and services through the quality function deployment process, you'll find—as have Quality Age firms the world over—that the design cycle is cut, at a minimum, in half. The design of the product or service is much more consistent with customer expectations. It is also compatible with the process itself.

Steady Improvement in the Quality Image

As your ongoing surveys of customers and prospects will show, your improvement program should steadily improve your firm's quality image. There will be other indicators, too, including increases in repeat business and referral business.

Those are three important ways that you'll know your transformation is under way. At the same time, you'll start to experience increased sales, profits, and improved competitive position.

But those traditional signs of success flow from increased energy and dynamism, reductions in "doing it over," and a steady improvement in your quality image—not the other way around.

Conclusion: Getting Better at Getting Better

As I write this chapter, the network news broadcasts are saturated with coverage of the funeral of Japan's late emperor Hirohito.

The theme seems to be "Japan in a new era," and the picture we're getting is fascinating, especially when you compare it with the old newsreel photos of Japan in 1945.

Back then, Japan was a destitute, defeated island nation, at the political and economic mercy of the world. Today, it's the world's third-largest economic power and America's principal banker. And all this happened in a country lacking in natural resources, with a territory only as large as the state of Montana and a population fully half the size of ours—in just 44 years.

The Japanese achieved turnaround and resurgence because they had the will to do it and the ability to persevere, year in and year out. They did it by methods of operation that are consistent with the culture of their people. Most of all, they did it by taking to heart certain tools and methods. But these tools and methods were *not* invented by Japanese; they were invented by Americans and taught *not* by other Japanese, but by American experts like Drs. Deming, Juran, and others.

The Japanese were like a dazed boxer, back to the canvas, with the count at nine. They had nowhere to go but up. They accepted the teaching partly because it made sense to them and partly because there was no harm in trying it. And they did more. They analyzed the tools, applied them, refined them, reshaped them, made them better and better.

160

In this, the Japanese have always excelled. Generally, where Americans have traditionally excelled at invention and innovation, the Japanese have traditionally excelled at refinement, at taking what already exists, and making it better.

By discussing the Japanese resurgence, I'm not for a moment suggesting that we simply import their system and install it here. Our cultural heritage precludes that, for one thing. I'm also not suggesting that American business today is analogous to the condition of the Japanese nation at the end of World War II. We've taken some hits, we have big problems, but we're still Number One. America has always survived stagnation and achieved new heights—and we'll do so again.

I bring up the example of Japan to show what can be done with the tools and, most of all, with the will.

If your business is in trouble today, you can turn it around. The example of Japan is clear and indisputable. So are numerous American examples such as the Ford Motor Company and Chrysler. If they can do it, why can't you?

If your business is excelling—the undisputed Number One in its field—you can always do even better! Why shouldn't you? When a football team wins the Super Bowl, its players don't sit back, rest on their laurels, and say, "We're the best, we don't need to get better for next year." They keep trying to get better, because they know that their opposition will get better and make every effort to knock this year's world champions off.

Today's top firms think exactly the same way. They haven't rested on their laurels; in their never-ending effort to stay on top, they've been among the first to adopt the principles of scientific improvement.

- Dupont-Vespel in Wilmington is one of the most dynamic users of SPC and design of experiments that I've ever worked with.

- The Federal-Mogul plant in Lancaster, Pennsylvania, implemented SPC and other IQM techniques very early and with marked enthusiasm.

- An executive from Swift-Eckrich, who has attended several of my seminars, told me, "No question that we have to implement these things. Our objective is to stay ahead of everyone else."

- Johnson Wax, under the direction of Sam Johnson, was one of the earliest firms to implement the IQM program, and they're still at it.
- Another executive, from Amoco, was even more blunt: "No way am I going to let my competitors get into this before we do."

I've noticed the same kind of thinking at Ford Motor Company. They've just chalked up their third year of industry-leading, record profits, but they haven't relaxed their improvement efforts. In fact, they've intensified them. While all the Big Three now have quality programs for their suppliers, only Ford requires that its suppliers earn Ford quality certification as a condition of continuing to do business with the firm.

And Ford has just replaced its original supplier program, called Q1 (which industry analysts feel is the toughest and most exacting of all automaker supplier programs) with an even tougher one called Total Quality Excellence. GM and Chrysler are also intensifying their supplier programs, and Johnson Wax has just initiated one called Guaranteed Quality Supplier.

The imperiled firms improve in order to survive; the top firms improve in order to stay ahead. In between are the firms that are hovering between disaster and leadership. These are the firms that not only haven't learned how to get better, they also seem to be afraid to.

Once, at one of my recent seminars, I polled the 34 attendees about their improvement philosophy. Of those 34 attendees—representing Fortune 200 firms—14 told me that their corporate policy was *not* to improve. The consensus was that the unions would not let them increase efficiency because of the fear of losing jobs.

I was incredulous. "You mean, you're locked into being inefficient the rest of your lives?"

"Absolutely," one of them answered.

If that's really their attitude, then they might as well close up shop right now—because everyone else is trying to get better.

Even Japan, our acknowledged nemesis, is feeling the heat—not from us, but from Taiwan and Korea and other Pacific Rim countries. Japan's domestic market share in textiles, cameras, and other items is eroding steadily. One Japanese government official, quoted in a recent *Wall Street Journal* report, said, "We're beginning to ride the same boat as the United States."[13]

No matter where you are today, you must get better. No matter where you are today, you can always get better. You can do that by implementing the principles that I've described in this book, the principles responsible for the success of today's Quality Age firms: the principles of Integrated Quality Management.

1. *Strive to improve customer perception of quality as well as the intrinsic quality of your product or service.* You can make the greatest product or service in the world, but if the *perception*, or *image*, of your firm's quality is terrible, your business will suffer just as much as if your product or service were mediocre.

   Sloppy, negative advertising and rude, indifferent salespeople are obvious contributors to a negative quality image. But so too are slovenly delivery people, poorly maintained company vehicles or facilities, inattentive receptionists, error-riddled documents, low worker morale, and more.

   No question, your quality image is shaped in part by the intrinsic quality of your product or service. But intrinsic quality is only part of the story. The rest of the input comes from the other aspects of your firm that touch people's lives.

   This is so important that I advocate establishing a separate department within your firm—a sort of quality department charged with monitoring your firm's quality image.

2. *In cost-of-quality calculations, include the cost of lost business.* Accountants like to total the cost of scrap, rework, and warranty expenses—plus the cost of inspection, training, and other quality initiatives—to establish the cost of

quality to the penny. The true cost of quality includes much more: the cost of lost business, when people won't buy a product from you again, or any other product you ever introduce; plus the marketing costs attendant to replacing those customers with new ones.

It's essential that you track the *true* cost of quality and make it known to all concerned.

3. *Define quality as exceeding customer expectations.* Quality is, in fact, a relationship between *what the customers expect to receive* and the *customers' perception of the value of what they received.* Perception, performance, and price are all critical components of what we generically call quality.

The key is finding the optimal mix of those components. It varies significantly among products or services and markets. The right mix is, therefore, a detailed description specific to the particular product or service. I call it the *customer goal.*

Moreover, the customer goal is *constantly changing.* We live in a dynamic, ever-changing world; the customer goal is dynamic and ever-changing, and we must, in response, be dynamic ourselves.

Your aim is threefold: (1) to identify today's customer goal in all its detail and complexity; (2) to identify its changes as they occur; (3) to develop the ability to *anticipate* changes before they occur.

"Meeting customer requirements" is the stale, stagnant language of yesterday. The customer goal is the dynamic language of today and tomorrow.

4. *Treat productivity as a subset of quality.* Quality and productivity are not antithetical. They are inseparable components of the customer satisfaction equation. Productivity is part of what makes value possible, in terms of the price to the customer.

In all your improvement efforts, you cannot sacrifice productivity in favor of quality, because productivity is in fact *part* of quality. The key to creating a balanced relationship between the two, and ensuring improvement, is to implement a scorekeeping method that takes both into account, that creates a common index, which I call the *quality/productivity index*.

5. *Bring entrepreneurial methods to your firm.* Today's entrepreneur is ultimately an expert communicator. The entrepreneur maintains intimate contact with the customer: listening, interpreting, reacting constantly. The entrepreneur also maintains intimate contact with the process, swiftly translating what is learned from the customer into meaningful and positive changes and adjustments to the process.

   By identifying and staying in contact with the customer goal, you can recreate the entrepreneurial spirit externally. You can recreate it internally by translating the customer goal into your process. Step by step, you must convert the customer goal into product or service features and technical requirements, so that what you produce and deliver matches the prevailing customer goal. By doing so, you also create, within your process, a series of supplier-customer relationships, as well as venues of communication that reinforce the entrepreneurial spirit.

6. *Recognize that suppliers are an integral part of your own business.* Quality starts with the products or services you acquire from outsiders. If the quality of those supplied items is poor or inconsistent, your own internal improvement efforts are doomed before they even start.

   You must, therefore, view your suppliers as partners— as, in fact, integral components of your own process. This philosophy precludes purchasing supplied products purely on the basis of price, which in turn precludes the use of multiple suppliers for any given product or service.

   Implementing close partnership relationships with sole-source suppliers, where practical, rewards both sides with benefits in costs, efficiency, research and development, and competitive strength.

7. *Implement scientific scorekeeping systems in the process.* Today's complex processes generate masses of information and data. Often we get hopelessly lost in our efforts

to refine and interpret this data and to find out *where we are*, which we must do before we can find out where we're headed.

Just as every firm utilizes meticulous methods to keep track of its finances, every firm must utilize scientific methods to generate and interpret meaningful data.

I call this *scorekeeping*, and there are several proven and simple methods to keep score on the process, including Statistical Process Control, design of experiments, and the quality/productivity index.

Effective scientific scorekeeping provides us with a window to the operation and gives us a clear, honest view of what is really happening. Effective scientific scorekeeping enables us to react to changes on an informed basis. Effective scientific scorekeeping is, in and of itself, a superior motivator and serves as the basis for positive reward and incentive programs.

Effective scorekeeping is at the heart of Integrated Quality Management and at the heart of improvement itself.

For too long, many stagnant firms have resisted change and fought to stay the same.

This is a hopeless notion, for change is the one constant. Left to themselves, things can only get worse. On the other hand, things can get better—starting with a change in mindset; with an acknowledgment of change; with a willingness to take charge, adjust goals ever upward, and work endlessly for improvement.

There's no such thing as an instant transition. It takes time. We go by inches. No Olympic gold medal winner began to train the week before the games.

In the final analysis, we have to learn to get better at getting better.

That, I submit, is an art—which we can all master when we begin to practice the science of keeping score.

References

1. J. M. Juran. *Juran on Planning For Quality* (New York: The Free Press, 1988), p. 148.
2. William W. Scherkenbach. *The Deming Route to Quality and Productivity* (Washington, D.C.: CEEPRess Books, 1986), p. 6.
3. Philip B. Crosby. *Quality is Free* (New York: NAL Penguin, Inc., 1979)
4. Genichi Taguchi. *System of Experimental Design* (White Plains, NY: UNIPUB/KRAUS International Publications, 1987), p. xxviii.
5. Peter Collier and David Horowitz. *The Fords: An American Epic* (New York: Summit Books, 1987), p. 120.
6. Collier and Horowitz. p. 123.
7. Thomas S. Monaghan, with Robert Anderson. *Pizza Tiger* (New York: Random House, 1986), p. 268.
8. Monaghan. p. 329.
9. Monaghan. p. 132.
10. Monaghan. p. 164.
11. W. Edwards Deming. *Out of the Crisis* (Cambridge: MIT Center for Advanced Engineering Studies, 1986), p. ix.
12. Monaghan. p. 18.
13. Damon Darlin. "Japan Is Getting a Dose of What It Gave U.S.: Low-Priced Imports," *The Wall Street Journal*, July 20, 1988, p. 1.

About the Author

Perry L. Johnson is President of Perry Johnson, Inc., a consulting firm specializing in integrating statistical process controls into working environments. The firm's client list contains over 7,500 firms, including 85 percent of the *Fortune* 500. Johnson received his undergraduate degree in mathematics from the University of Illinois and graduate training in statistics from the University of Detroit.